Spiritual Tweezers

Removing Paul's "Thorn in the Flesh" and Other
False Objections to God's Will for Healing

SECOND EDITION
REVISED & EXPANDED

Art Thomas

SUPERNATURAL TRUTH PRODUCTIONS, LLC
Practical Training for Spirit-Filled Living
www.SupernaturalTruth.com

Copyright © 2013, 2016 Art Thomas

SECOND EDITION, REVISED AND UPDATED

Please note that Supernatural Truth Productions, LLC, chooses to capitalize various pronouns and metaphors used for the Father, the Son, and the Holy Spirit, even when such capitalization does not exist in an original source, including Bible translations. This is a style decision made for the sake of honoring God in our text.

ISBN-10: 0692624473
ISBN-13: 978-0692624470

Dedication

I dedicate this book to the many dearly loved children of God who have been taught that their physical healing isn't God's will. You've lived with injustice long enough, and I'm thrilled to say that God has a greater plan.

This book is your invitation to encounter the Father who loves you and has your best interests in mind.

SPIRITUAL TWEEZERS – Art Thomas

Acknowledgements

I would like to express a special word of thanks to my amazing wife, Robin, who continually supports my ministry and time spent with God. If not for her faithfulness to me and to our boys, I would never have the time or freedom to write anything at all. All my writing is more of a testament to her hard work than it is to mine.

SPIRITUAL TWEEZERS – Art Thomas

Endorsements

I love this book! It's a simple read, but powerful. If you have ever struggled with the thought of having a sickness or disease caused by a thorn in the flesh, you have to read this book. *Spiritual Tweezers* is a must-have in your arsenal against the forces of darkness. Win!

> - Pete Cabrera Jr.
> *Royal Family International University*

The miraculous testimonies I have from traveling with Art Thomas are often met with unbelief. My eyes have been blessed as I've watched whole rooms of people healed as the body of Christ ministered to each other. The same caution and unbelief that I often encounter when relating these stories is what Art honestly and gracefully targets in *Spiritual Tweezers*. With clarity and pithy humor, Art gives careful, honest, and inspiring answers to common objections to healing theology. *Spiritual Tweezers* overflows with hope for those struggling with divine healing in either intellect or body.

> - Jonathan Ammon
> *Urban Missionary and Ministry Associate of Art Thomas*
> *Hamtramck, Michigan*

I have had the privilege of ministering with Art for several years, and his message is the same everywhere we go: Jesus paid the price. This message, along with his love of Scripture, makes *Spiritual Tweezers* a great read for anyone struggling with questions about healing theology and for those desiring to see Jesus receive all that He paid for.

> - James Loruss
> *Vice President of Wildfire Ministries International*

SPIRITUAL TWEEZERS – Art Thomas

Table of Contents:

PART TWO – Other Objections to God's will for Healing

PART THREE – Ten Things Jesus NEVER Said about Healing

Foreword

TO THE FIRST EDITION
BY JOSHUA GREESON

O ne of the subjects I am personally most passionate about is God's desire for every person to be healed and healthy. For me, healing is not about the "flash" (although God sure does put on some good shows, to be sure). In my opinion, healing (and our theology for it) is important because it draws a picture of the God we believe in.

What someone believes about God's will concerning healing says a lot about the nature of the God they follow. If someone believes that God gives people cancer to teach them something, for instance, that's a cruel god. If another believes that God sometimes wants to heal, but sometimes He doesn't, that's an inconsistent, wishy-washy god. If one believes that we couldn't possibly know what God wants to do in a situation, then that's a mysterious, unknowable, distant, impersonal god... and so on.

I don't know about you; but that's not the God I read about in Scripture. I read about a God who is Light, and in Him is no darkness at all (1 John 1:5). I read about a God who gives good and perfect gifts to us and never varies from this whatsoever (James 1:17). I read about a God who sticks to His promises, and it's impossible for Him to lie (Hebrews 6:18). I read about a God Who IS Love. Not just "has" love, or a God Who "loves," but a God Who IS Love (1 John 4:8). I read about a God who is steady, consistent, reliable, sure, and Who never changes (Malachi 3:6).

Thankfully, Art Thomas is reading the same Bible I'm reading and believes in the same God—the One Who is most clearly displayed through His Son, Jesus Christ. Jesus is God in the flesh and is the only perfect picture of the Father. He is the will of God incarnate. Jesus came to set the captives free (Luke 4:18). He "went about doing good and healing all who were oppressed by the devil" (Acts 10:38). Since Jesus is the same yesterday, today and forever (Hebrews 13:8), Jesus is still doing these things today.

It is arguable that a third or more of Jesus' earthly ministry time was spent healing the sick. As believers in union with Jesus, it's no longer us living, but Christ living through us (Galatians 2:20). Therefore, healing the sick should be a significant part of His ministry through us too. As a matter of fact, Jesus directly instructed His followers on more than one occasion to carry on healing the sick by the power of God. He hasn't changed His mind. Healing is our commission as ambassadors of Christ. Settling any questions or doubts—and knowing for sure God always wants us well—is an important step toward us representing Jesus more accurately to the world.

Art recognizes that well-meaning Christians over the centuries have developed ideas that, unintentionally, paint a very different picture of God than Jesus does. From a logical desire to explain unanswered questions, some have read the Bible through the lenses of grief and personal disappointment. In doing so, they have often misread the Bible to say that it's not always God's will to heal. They have latched on to anything that even hints that it might be OK for us to remain as we are—and not be challenged to grow up into Christ.

Anyone who steps out in ministering healing hears these same objections all the time... "If God wanted me well, then I wouldn't be sick," they say. "What about Paul's thorn?" they ask. "What about Job?" "What if God is trying to teach me something?" These questions and others like them have hindered believers from both receiving healing for themselves, and from stepping out and ministering healing to others in the authority of Jesus. It's time for this to stop!

We as Believers can't have ANY doubt that God wants us well if we hope to pursue healing for ourselves or anyone else. If we leave room in our thinking for the idea that sickness might ever be God's will, then we will only half-heartedly believe for healing. After all, if sickness might be God's will, then we might be fighting against God—and we definitely wouldn't want to do that! So instead, we innocently and ignorantly take a beating from the devil!

It is vitally important for Christians to forever crush these nagging questions if we intend to grow up in Jesus and reflect Him accurately to the world around us. In this book, the author assists us in doing just that. He makes a compelling case—eliminating these questions from our minds through an honest and insightful evaluation of key

Scripture passages on the subject. In most cases, Art offers several viable interpretations and lets the readers decide for themselves which one carries the most weight. He helps us to look at the Scriptures for what they actually say, rather than see them through the traditions of men that have been passed on for so long. More importantly than just a good argument, "the proof is in the pudding." Art's personal ministry proves out—time and time again—that God is good and kind, and wants people well.

Art settles these questions and practices what he preaches, and it's for this reason that I heartily endorse this book and his ministry. Do yourself (and those you minister to) a favor: Start reading, and let your mind be renewed by the word of God!

Joshua Greeson
Author, *God's Will is Always Healing*

Preface

TO THE SECOND EDITION

In 2009, after years of believing it was sometimes God's will to heal and sometimes not, I came to the difficult conclusion that I had been wrong. I had brought all my arguments to the Scriptures, and I watched them crumble one by one.

This book covers most of those arguments so that you too can benefit from a logical, sensible, sound examination of the Scriptures.

When I first published this book in 2013, it began as a response to an e-mail I had received that asked, "What about Paul's thorn in the flesh? God didn't heal Paul, and it was obviously His will for Paul to suffer in that way. I want to believe what you're teaching, but I just don't see a way around this issue."

As I worked through the Scriptures to produce a

meaningful answer, I found that my simple e-mail was becoming long enough to maybe be a blog article. But before I knew it, it had grown to the size of a small book.

I added a chapter that covered an assortment of other objections (now divided out and expanded as "Part Two") and published *Spiritual Tweezers* within the month.

During the three years since the release of that first edition, my experience has developed even further, and so has my teaching ministry. I've debated healing ministry with a lot of really smart people, which has refined my arguments for God's will to heal. I've endured multiple "firing-lines" of Q&A sessions at ministry events throughout the United States. I've filmed, interviewed, and hung out with healing ministers from around the world, picking their brains and discussing the nuances of Biblical interpretation as it relates to healing. I released a movie about healing ministry—*Paid in Full*—that has been distributed around the world and even aired to millions on GodTV. I've even been blessed with multiple TV and radio appearances, opening up my assertions to the scrutiny of a massive audience. And I've taken the time to study and examine the Scriptures even closer than before.

I still have yet to hear any argument that successfully causes me to question my conviction that God's will is always to heal.

In 2016, I decided the experiences of the last three years needed to come to bear on the content of this book. With a fresh facelift on the book's format and design, plus a tweak of the content and an addition of an all new section, the finished product now rests in your hands. I have tried as much as possible to maintain the original appeal of the first book, which was the fact that it was a fast read with simple, straightforward arguments that anyone could understand and use. My hope is that this will be an even more useful reference for those who want to convince their Christian friends of God's will to heal, and perhaps it will be used to awaken even more people to the unmistakable reality of this glorious truth.

I'm excited to see the fruit of the new segment (found in Part Three). On January 26, 2014, I preached a sermon in Jackson, Michigan, titled "Ten Things Jesus Never Said about Healing." As I write today, the video of that sermon has been viewed almost 15,000 times, and I was even asked to re-hash the material for a local television show that aired along much of Florida's Gulf Coast. Given the popularity of this message and how closely it connects with the message of this book, I thought it would be good to include the material here for all my readers. It too has been revised and expanded from its original sermon form, bringing it up to speed with everything I have learned and experienced since originally preaching it.

I pray this book is a blessing to you as you search the Scriptures and discover the reality that God's will is ALWAYS to heal.

Be blessed,

Art Thomas
www.ArtThomas.org

SPIRITUAL TWEEZERS – Art Thomas

PART

Eliminating
Paul's Thorn in the Flesh

SPIRITUAL TWEEZERS – Art Thomas

Introduction to Part One

I am convinced that it is always (yes, 100% of the time) God's will to heal every sickness, disease, deformity, pain, injury, or other physical problem. And if you've followed my ministry for any length of time, you know I'm vocal about it.

Understandably, this passion (for Jesus to receive everything for which He paid) attracts some intense arguments from the other side. One of the most common is this: **"What about Paul's thorn in the flesh?"**

According to these naysayers, God gave Paul a sickness or disease of some kind to keep him humble; and God refused to heal Paul of that condition. Naturally, this leads to many people wondering if their own condition might be a thorn in the flesh—something given by God to keep them humble.

In this opening portion of this book, I want to put to rest the misunderstandings surrounding Paul's mysterious "thorn" and prove that it was not a physical disease, or an eye problem, or anything of the sort. But most importantly, I want to prove that it is not a valid excuse for people to remain sick.

Jesus deserves to receive everything for which He paid. He deserves to be known for who He is and not misunderstood because of one obscure passage. Like Paul, I want to "demolish arguments and every pretension that sets itself up against the knowledge of God." (See 2 Corinthians 10:5.)

Because this topic is so deeply rooted in the hearts and minds of so many, I believe it deserves more than a haphazard answer. Consequently, this is a rather lengthy study of a mere three scripture verses—not because I have to do a lot of intellectual gymnastics to "make my theory work," but because there is so much evidence to support this perspective, and it's all worth sharing.

Let's start by looking at the passage where Paul introduced us to his infamous "thorn in the flesh:"

> **2 Corinthians 12:7-10** – And lest I should be exalted above measure by the abundance of the revelations, a thorn in the flesh was given to me, a messenger of Satan to buffet me, lest I be exalted above measure. Concerning this thing I pleaded with the Lord three times that it might depart from me. And He said to me, "My grace is sufficient for you, for My strength is made perfect in weakness." Therefore most gladly I will rather boast in my

> infirmities, that the power of Christ may rest
> upon me. Therefore I take pleasure in
> infirmities, in reproaches, in needs, in
> persecutions, in distresses, for Christ's sake.
> For when I am weak, then I am strong. (NKJV)

There are seven important questions raised by this scripture that must be answered before we can adequately put this matter to rest:

1. What was the "abundance of revelations" to which Paul referred?
2. Was Paul speaking literally or figuratively about his "thorn in the flesh"?
3. What is meant by the term "messenger of Satan"?
4. What is meant by the word "buffet"?
5. Does it make sense that Paul would plead for God to take away a sickness?
6. What does it mean for God's grace to be sufficient?
7. Is it Biblically sound to take pleasure in sickness and disease?

Before we dive into these questions, I need to settle the most popular argument: that Paul's thorn in the flesh was an eye problem. Then we'll dive into those seven questions. And once those seven things are settled, I want to share with you my own personal experience with a "thorn in the flesh." Finally, I'll offer instructions and encouragement for anyone who is presently dealing with a thorn in the flesh; and I'll also take a moment to instruct those who have realized throughout the course of this book that their condition is not actually a thorn in the flesh and that God wants to heal them!

Since this book was first published, a handful of people have told me that they were healed while reading, including a good friend of mine. My expectation is that many more will be healed as they read this book—not only physically healed, but also emotionally and intellectually as the truth of Jesus' power and will to heal is clearly revealed through Scripture.

It's time to remove Paul's thorn from the lineup of arguments against God's will to heal. Here come some spiritual tweezers!

Was Paul's Thorn in the Flesh an Eye Problem?

One of the most popular theories about Paul's thorn in the flesh is that it was an eye problem. The stance is taken from two passages in particular, both from the same letter:

> **Galatians 4:13-15 –** You know that because of physical infirmity I preached the gospel to you at the first. And my trial which was in my flesh you did not despise or reject, but you received me as an angel of God, even as Christ Jesus. What then was the blessing you enjoyed? For I bear you witness that, if possible, you would have plucked out your own eyes and given them

to me. (NKJV)

Galatians 6:11 — See with what large letters I
have written to you with my own hand! (NKJV)

Paul's Physical Infirmity

Let's take care of the first passage first. Paul makes it
clear that it was because of "physical infirmity" that he
preached the Gospel "at first" to the Galatians. So if we
want to see what physical infirmity Paul is referring to, we
should turn to the book of Acts and examine Paul's first
missionary journey throughout the region of Galatia.

It is important to note that Galatia was not a city but
rather a large region that contained several cities, including
Lystra, Iconium, and Derbe. The first time we see Paul
reaching this region is with Barnabas in Pisidian Antioch; but
at this time, they were ministering to the Jews. That,
however, didn't turn out so well:

Acts 13:50-51 — But the Jewish leaders incited
the God-fearing women of high standing and
the leading men of the city. They stirred up
persecution against Paul and Barnabas, and
expelled them from their region. So they shook
the dust off their feet as a warning to them and
went to Iconium. (NIV)

After being rejected by the Jews of Pisidian Antioch,
Paul and Barnabas turned their sights to the Gentiles. (See
Acts 13:46-48.) And these "uncircumcised" Gentiles were
the ones to whom Paul wrote his letter. (See Galatians 6:12.)
These are the ones to whom he wrote when he said, "You
know that because of physical infirmity I preached the

gospel to you at the first." (See Galatians 4:13.)

What physical infirmity did Paul have when he visited the Gentiles of Galatia? First, let's look at the Greek. The word for "physical" here is "*sarx*," which is the same word translated elsewhere as "flesh." And the word for "infirmity" used here is "*astheneia*"—the same word translated as "weakness" in 2 Corinthians 11 to refer to persecution. (See 2 Corinthians 11:23-27, and specifically verse 30.)

So the term "physical infirmity" could just as validly be translated "weakness of the flesh." And given the way Paul is known to have used the word "*astheneia*" (weakness or infirmity) in reference to persecution, it is sensible to consider that Paul was likely referring to (1) the persecution he endured from the Jews before coming to the Gentiles of Galatia, or (2) possibly his resulting physical condition after having endured that persecution. (See Acts 13:50-51.)

Paul didn't only use the term "weakness of the flesh" but also "trial."

> **Galatians 4:14** – And my trial which was in my flesh you did not despise or reject, but you received me as an angel of God, even as Christ Jesus. (NKJV)

It would have been easy for the Galatian Christians to "despise or reject" the trial of persecution Paul was physically enduring. Consider what took place as he ministered in Iconium:

> **Acts 14:4-7** – The people of the city were divided; some sided with the Jews, others with the apostles. There was a plot afoot among both

Gentiles and Jews, together with their leaders,
to mistreat them and stone them. But they
found out about it and fled to the Lycaonian
cities of Lystra and Derbe and to the
surrounding country, where they continued to
preach the gospel. (NIV)

Anyone wanting to simply avoid conflict could have
rejected Paul rather than receiving him and his divisive
message.

In fact, there is some disagreement among translators
as to whether the word "trial" was pointed at Paul or the
Galatians. For example, while the New King James Version
reads "trial which was in my flesh," the New American
Standard Bible renders as follows:

Galatians 4:14 – and that which was a trial to
you in my bodily condition you did not despise
or loathe, but you received me as an angel of
God, as Christ Jesus Himself. (NASB)

In this case, Paul's bodily condition (likely due to the
persecution suffered in Pisidian Antioch) was said to be a
trial to the Galatians (not simply a trial to himself).

Whether it was Paul's trial or the Galatians' trial isn't
actually important. The point is that either way, the book of
Acts offers us the context of persecution, which is consistent
with Paul's use of the Greek word "*astheneia*" (translated
"infirmity" or "weakness").

Friends, Romans, Countrymen: Lend Me Your Eyes

With those things settled, we still need to provide a response to verse 15:

> **Galatians 4:15** – What then was the blessing you enjoyed? For I bear you witness that, if possible, you would have plucked out your own eyes and given them to me. (NKJV)

Why would Paul say that the Galatians would have given him their eyes if he didn't have an eye problem? There are two possible answers: (1) it was a figure of speech, or (2) he actually had an eye problem.

Consider, briefly, the first option. In America, we have some gruesome sayings of our own. For example, we might say that something cost us "an arm and a leg." Or one might say, "He's such a good friend, I would give my right arm for him."

Admittedly, though, to form this argument, we should ideally find contemporary uses of such a figure of speech in the literature of the day. Unfortunately, I'm not a student of first-century, secular Greek literature, so I don't have much to go on here. So while this is possible, it's not necessarily the case.

A second possibility, though, is that something was actually wrong with Paul's eyes. And given what we've seen in the book of Acts, it is plausible that something happened to his eyes during the persecution.

Another thing that happened during Paul's visit to the towns of Galatia was that he was stoned, which certainly could have severely bruised his face and eyes. (See Acts 14:19-20.) This, by the way, happened just before he returned to Pisidian Antioch, which is more in the heart of Galatia. This is the place where he and Barnabas had been rejected by the Jews when they first began preaching in Galatia, which means that this return trip could be what Paul was referring to when he said "at first."

Look at Those Letters!

We have yet one more loose end to tie up, though: What about Paul's big handwriting? (See Galatians 6:11.)

There are two possibilities that do not necessarily have anything to do with an eye problem: (1) The persecution Paul endured had hindered his fine motor skills, or (2) Paul was actually referring to other letters.

The first possibility is rather self-explanatory. Years of stonings, whippings, beatings, and other trials could have left his hands mildly impaired. In this case, it wouldn't be easy for him to write small text.

While I personally subscribe to this first possibility, the second option also deserves an honorable mention. In English, the word "letter" could refer to "letters of the alphabet" or also to "letters of correspondence." The same is true in the Greek. The word used for "letters" here is *"gramma,"* from which we derive the word "grammar," and it pertains to any sort of writing (from individual letters all the way up to entire books).

On one hand, we have a Biblical example of this word meaning "letters of the alphabet":

Luke 23:38 – And an inscription also was written over Him in letters [*gramma*] of Greek, Latin,

and Hebrew: THIS IS THE KING OF THE JEWS.
(NKJV)

And on the other hand, we have a Biblical example of this word meaning "letters of correspondence":

> **Acts 28:21** – Then they said to him, "We neither received letters [*gramma*] from Judea concerning you, nor have any of the brethren who came reported or spoken any evil of you. (NKJV)

While most translations of Galatians 6:11 prefer to interpret that Paul wrote large letters of the alphabet, it is interesting to note that the King James renders the text, "Ye see how large a letter I have written unto you with mine own hand." Similarly, some have argued that the "letters" to which Paul referred may have been personal letters that accompanied the main letter to the Galatians, and these may have been written in his own handwriting.

Again, I personally lean toward the explanation of persecution. When a person has an eye problem, they may have an easier time *reading* large letters, but they do not necessarily *write* with large letters. So the fact that Paul wrote large letters is more likely a problem with fine motor skills than a problem with vision.

Oh, Those Pitiful Eyes

Finally, if I may beat a dead horse once more, we need to ask what kind of eye problem the proponents of this view believe Paul had. If it was merely impaired vision, I would hardly call that "a messenger of Satan sent to buffet me."

As a matter of fact, the proponents of the "eye problem" argument tend to lean toward something more sinister – something contagious that involves pus oozing from the eyes: Ophthalmia.

F.F. Bosworth (1877-1958) wrote an extensive rebuttal to this assertion in his classic book *Christ the Healer*. The argument for the eye problem came from a pastor in New York who published a printed sermon on the matter and distributed it to everyone in the vicinity of Bosworth's meetings there. A portion of that clergyman's letter reads as follows:

> The fact is, Paul was sick. He was the sickest of men. He had one of the worst and most painful of oriental diseases. He had ophthalmia, a disease of the eyes. The proof that he had it is overwhelming. He tells us that he had a "thorn in the flesh." When Paul stood before Christians, his eyes filled with unspeakable pus, unspeakable matter running down over his face. Why would they have gouged out their eyes for him except that his eyes, as he stood before them, were a pitiable...sight to them...? The particular pain of this disease is that it is like a "stake" in the eyes. It is beyond dispute that Paul was a sick man... (Bosworth, *Christ the Healer,* Revell, 2007, pages 193-194.)

Bosworth proceeds to pick apart the man's argument. Some of the things I have written throughout this article were first gleaned from Bosworth's writings here and polished through personal experience and my own study of Scripture. Of particular interest, though, are the points he makes specifically against the idea of such a hideous eye disease.

Bosworth asserts:

> Suppose our brother is correct in stating that Paul was the "sickest of men," suffering with ophthalmia, is it not strange that when the Ephesians saw the pus running from Paul's eyes and found that God would not heal him, this sight gave them faith for "special miracles" to be wrought on their behalf? It is stated here, "God wrought special miracles by the hands of Paul: so that from his body were brought unto the sick handkerchiefs or aprons, and the diseases departed from them, and the evil spirits went out of them" (Acts 19:11-12)...Today, if handkerchiefs were brought from one suffering with ophthalmia, rather than laying them on the sick for healing, we would burn them to keep from spreading the infection. (Bosworth, *Christ the Healer,* Revell, 2007, page 201.)

Bosworth makes several other great points about Paul's effective healing ministry and the faith he inspired in others, which would not have made sense if "unspeakable pus" was oozing from his eyes.

By now, it should be clear that while it's possible and plausible that Paul may have suffered some sort of short-term injury to his eyes after persecution in Galatia, there is not sufficient evidence that Paul had an eye disease of any kind—and it is certainly unlikely (in the light of Scripture) that Paul had such a horrible condition as ophthalmia!

Having eliminated this argument from the equation, we now must move on to more relevant matters. What was Paul's thorn in the flesh? Why did he receive it? What was its purpose? These questions and more will be addressed in the rest of this teaching.

Question 1

What Was the "Abundance of Revelations" to which Paul Referred?

Paul said that his thorn in the flesh was a direct response to the "abundance of revelations" he had received. That's important because it implies that not everyone is a candidate for a thorn in the flesh. If we can identify the "abundance of revelations" as the source or reason for Paul's thorn, then we can immediately eliminate billions of people from the list of possible recipients.

These revelations are clearly described in the previous verses. Here's the passage in the New Living Translation:

> **2 Corinthians 12:1-7 –** This boasting will do no good, but I must go on. I will reluctantly tell about visions and revelations from the Lord. I

was caught up to the third heaven fourteen years ago. Whether I was in my body or out of my body, I don't know—only God knows. Yes, only God knows whether I was in my body or outside my body. But I do know that I was caught up to paradise and heard things so astounding that they cannot be expressed in words, things no human is allowed to tell.

That experience is worth boasting about, but I'm not going to do it. I will boast only about my weaknesses. If I wanted to boast, I would be no fool in doing so, because I would be telling the truth. But I won't do it, because I don't want anyone to give me credit beyond what they can see in my life or hear in my message, even though I have received such wonderful revelations from God. So to keep me from becoming proud, I was given a thorn in my flesh, a messenger from Satan to torment me and keep me from becoming proud. (NLT)

Been to Heaven Lately?

Healing evangelist Smith Wigglesworth (1859-1947) once encountered a woman who was terribly twisted up with rheumatism. He asked her, "What makes you lie here?"

"I've come to the conclusion," she replied, "that I have a thorn in the flesh."

Wigglesworth was known for his bluntness, and he certainly followed through with his reputation in this situation! Upon hearing the woman's answer, he responded, "To what wonderful degree of righteousness have you attained that you must have a thorn in the flesh? Have you had such an abundance of divine revelations that there is a danger of your being exalted above measure?" (Wigglesworth, *Greater Works: Experiencing God's Power,* Whitaker House, 1999, page 136.)

Dr. T.L. Osborn (1923-2013) wrote, "Paul's own reason for his thorn excludes practically everyone else. You should not claim that your sickness was a thorn like Paul's unless you, too, have received such an abundance of revelations that you need to be kept from being exalted." (Osborn, *Healing the Sick,* Harrison House, Inc., 1992, page 204.)

Regardless of what Paul's "thorn in the flesh" actually is, if you've never had intense revelations like Paul, then you're probably exempt from having the same condition. To be intellectually honest, though, I suppose there could be other reasons for a person receiving a thorn in the flesh, but you'll be hard-pressed to find one in the Bible.

Question 2
Was Paul Speaking Literally or Figuratively about His "Thorn in the Flesh"?

The term "thorn in the flesh" is either literal, figurative, or a combination of the two.

Just How Literal was that Thorn?

If it's a literal thorn in his literal flesh, then asking God to take it away doesn't make sense. All Paul needed was a pair of tweezers (which arguably existed in Rome at the time) or at least a knife to cut it out himself! For that matter, I don't think I've ever known someone to call a splinter a "messenger of Satan sent to torment me." That must have been some thorn!

Furthermore, if thorns make us spiritually stronger, why don't we all just roll around in some rose bushes until we're supercharged with glory? I think you see the point: the term "thorn in the flesh" cannot be completely literal.

What did Paul mean by "Flesh"?

Another perspective is that the term "thorn" was figurative while the term "flesh" was literal. In this case, the so-called "thorn" could be any sort of affliction or problem that directly affected Paul's actual "flesh" and also fit the description of being a "messenger of Satan."

What about the word "flesh?" In the original Greek, the word used for "flesh" here is "*sarx*," which does, in fact, refer to the human body (specifically the "meat" of the body beneath the skin, according to *Strong's Greek Dictionary*). It also can refer, however, to the figurative human element of a person—like when Paul wrote about the "carnal [*sarx*] mind." (See Romans 8:7.)

Let's think logically about this for a moment. First, as you'll see in the next chapter, the term "messenger of Satan" literally refers to a demon. So if Paul's "thorn" was actually a demon (as I agree that it was), and if the word "flesh" literally means his physical body, then we have to figure out how a demon could be "in" his body.

Paul argued that the Christian's body is a temple of the Holy Spirit. (See 1 Corinthians 6:19.) A few verses earlier, he asked, "For what do righteousness and wickedness have in common? Or what fellowship can light have with darkness?" (See verse 14.) While it's true that demons can influence Spirit-filled Christians, it is also true that they can only influence from the outside. And if they can only influence from the outside, then Paul could not have a demon "in" his body. Thus the half-figurative, half-literal interpretation causes too many theological issues to make sense biblically.

Paul: Master of Jewish Metaphor

The last possibility is that the entire term "thorn in the flesh" is figurative. Biblically speaking, this is a sensible conclusion. Consider the following examples of similar figures of speech:

> **Numbers 33:55** – But if you do not drive out the inhabitants of the land, those you allow to remain will become **barbs in your eyes** and **thorns in your sides**. They will give you trouble in the land where you will live. (NIV, emphasis added)

> **Joshua 23:12-13** – But if you turn away and ally yourselves with the survivors of these nations that remain among you and if you intermarry with them and associate with them, then you may be sure that the Lord your God will no longer drive out these nations before you. Instead, they will become snares and traps for you, **whips on your backs** and **thorns in your eyes**, until you perish from this good land, which the Lord your God has given you. (NIV, emphasis added)

Here we find four purely figurative terms: (1) barbs in your eyes, (2) thorns in your sides, (3) whips on your backs, and (4) thorns in your eyes. In none of these cases are the terms literal. They're also not partially figurative and partially literal (can you imagine a Canaanite sticking out of an

Israelite's eye socket?).

Paul was a religiously devoted "Hebrew of Hebrews" before his conversion, so it wouldn't be a stretch for him to use a purely figurative term that was reminiscent of similar terms in the Old Testament.

In none of the four cases did the expression pertain to a sickness or disease. Rather, in all four cases, the expression referred to aggravating persons who would cause problems and frustration for the people of God.

Paul said that his "thorn in the flesh" was a "messenger of Satan" sent "to buffet me." Paul described his "thorn in the flesh" as an aggravating personality of some sort that brought repeated trouble to him. For this reason, we must now determine what is meant by the term "messenger of Satan."

Question 3
What is Meant by the Term "Messenger of Satan"?

The Greek word for "messenger" here is "*aggelos*" (pronounced "*ang'-el-os*").

- Three times, this word is used in the New Testament to refer to John the Baptist. (See Matthew 11:10, Mark 1:2, and Luke 7:27.)
- Once, it referred to John's disciples and once to Jesus' disciples (See Luke 7:24 and 9:53.)
- Once it referred to Joshua and Caleb when Rahab hid them. (See James 2:25.)
- And once it is used to refer to Paul's "thorn in the flesh."

But 178 times—the overwhelming majority—this Greek word is translated "angel," "angels," or "angel's." In these cases, the word specifically refers to spiritual beings, whether of God or of the devil.

Angels of Satan

For the sake of our text (in which the term "messenger [angel] of Satan" is used), consider the following scriptures:

Matthew 25:41 – Then he will say to those on his left, "Depart from me, you who are cursed, into the eternal fire prepared for the devil and his angels." (NIV)

Revelation 12:7-9 – Then war broke out in heaven. Michael and his angels fought against the dragon, and the dragon and his angels fought back. But he was not strong enough, and they lost their place in heaven. The great dragon was hurled down—that ancient serpent called the devil, or Satan, who leads the whole world astray. He was hurled to the earth, and his angels with him. (NIV)

In both these cases, the Greek word "*aggelos*," when associated with Satan, refers specifically to demonic spirits. These are "angels of Satan"—the very term applied to Paul's thorn in the flesh.

Another interesting thing to note is that when we read that Paul's thorn was "given" to him and that this "messenger of Satan" was "sent," we often assume that it was sent by God. However, this misconception isn't found in this passage. On the contrary, we have the term "messenger of Satan," which implies that the demon was "given by" or "sent by" Satan, not by God.

Satan and Self-Sabotage

"But," one might argue, "Paul's thorn in the flesh was sent to keep him humble. Why would the devil want to keep someone humble?" I won't pretend to understand why the devil so often works against himself, but this wouldn't be the only Scriptural instance of such a thing.

Consider First Corinthians 5:5, in which Paul prescribes, "...hand this man over to Satan for the destruction of the flesh, so that his spirit may be saved on the day of the Lord." Then there's First Timothy 1:20, which says, "Among them are Hymenaeus and Alexander, whom I have handed over to Satan to be taught not to blaspheme."

Satan destroys flesh; but it often brings people to salvation. Satan is a blasphemer, and yet he also somehow teaches people not to blaspheme.

While on one hand I would not suggest that Paul had been handed over to Satan in response to unrepentant sin in his life, we can still make a biblical case that Satan and his demons often play a (perhaps unwitting) role in human sanctification. It is therefore not a stretch to see Satan "give" a demon "lest" Paul become conceited.

Exalting the Flesh

As a final thought on this point, one popular author has pointed out that the King James renders Paul's words to read, "...lest I should be exalted above measure," rather than the NIV: "...in order to keep me from becoming

SPIRITUAL TWEEZERS — Art Thomas

conceited..." This teacher has suggested that Paul being exalted would have actually been a *good* thing (as in Matthew 23:12, Luke 14:11; 18:14; and 1 Peter 5:6, where God promises to exalt those who humble themselves). He suggests that the devil sent this demon to keep God from exalting Paul in a good way.

There are two problems with this perspective: (1) No demon can stop God, and (2) Paul's description of his thorn uses a different Greek word than the Scriptures where being exalted is used positively. The word used for "exalted" in the context of Paul's thorn is *"huperairomai,"* which refers specifically to self-exaltation rather than healthy exaltation. It is used only in one other passage in the New Testament—Second Thessalonians 2:4—and clearly has a different usage than the blessing of being exalted by God. On the other hand, the Scriptures where being exalted is positive use the word *"hupsoō."* The first word means to overly exalt while the second word means to be raised into right position. Paul used the first word, not the second, so his thorn truly was sent to keep him humble.

Question 4
What Does the Word "Buffet" Mean?

In the original Greek language, the word for "buffet" is "*kolaphizō*." This word specifically means "to strike with the fist." (See *Strong's* and *Thayer's*.) It is only used four other times in the Greek New Testament, and in all four cases, it clearly pertains to persecution:

> **Matthew 26:67-68** – Then they spit in his face and struck him with their fists [*kolaphizō*]. Others slapped him and said, "Prophesy to us, Messiah. Who hit you?"(NIV)

> **Mark 14:65** – Then some began to spit at him; they blindfolded him, struck him with their fists [*kolaphizō*], and said, "Prophesy!" And the

guards took him and beat him. (NIV)

1 Corinthians 4:11 – To this very hour we go hungry and thirsty, we are in rags, we are brutally treated [*kolaphizō*], we are homeless. (NIV)

1 Peter 2:19-20 – For it is commendable if someone bears up under the pain of unjust suffering because they are conscious of God. But how is it to your credit if you receive a beating [*kolaphizō*] for doing wrong and endure it? But if you suffer for doing good and you endure it, this is commendable before God. (NIV)

While the word specifically means a single blow of the fist, its context regularly implies repeated blows over a period of time. It implies "brutal treatment" and "beating." Interestingly, it is always used in the context of a person of some kind administering the blows, which further reinforces the fact of Paul's thorn in the flesh being a demon.

Furthermore, the way such beatings take place is through repeated forceful blows, not a single prolonged pain or pressure. So if an analogy is being drawn to sickness or disease, it would make more sense that it refers to something involving sudden-onset attacks rather than a long-term chronic condition.

Demons and Christians

At this point, it is important to realize what sort of things demons can do to attack (or buffet) people. I should first be clear, though, that demons cannot "possess"

Christians. The fruit of the Holy Spirit includes self-control. (See Galatians 5:22-23.) So for a demon to take over a Christian who is full of the Holy Spirit wouldn't be sensible.

Nevertheless, demons can certainly *influence* Christians. If they couldn't, then why would we need to put on the full armor of God? (See Ephesians 6:11.) Why would we need to take every thought captive? (See 2 Corinthians 10:5.) Why would we be reminded that we wrestle against demons rather than people? (See Ephesians 6:12.) Why would we be warned about demons deceiving Christians? (See 1 Timothy 4:1 and 1 John 4:1.) Why would we be instructed not to give the devil a foothold? (See Ephesians 4:27.) Why would Peter command us to be "alert and of sober mind" as a means of steering clear of the enemy? (See 1 Peter 5:8.)

While it is true that we have authority over demons, this doesn't mean that they pose no threat to us. The following is a biblical list of ways that demons can influence Christians:

- Demons can use others to discourage us. (See Matthew 16:23.)
- They can tempt us. (See Mark 1:13 and 1 Corinthians 7:5.)
- They can influence our emotions. (See 2 Timothy 1:7.)
- They can incite others to violence toward us. (See John 8:4; 13:2; Acts 13:8-10; and Revelation 2:10.)
- They can rob us of spiritual growth. (See Mark 4:15.)
- They can outwit us when our guard is down (See 2 Corinthians 2: 10-11.)
- They can use others to annoy us. (See Acts 16:16-18.)

- They can hinder our plans for kingdom work. (See 1 Thessalonians 2:18.)
- They move people into the Church with the goal of choking out life there. (See Matthew 13:37-39 and John 6:70-71.)
- And they can also cause physical problems. (See Luke 13:16.)

Any of these demonic actions could have been the mission of the spirit that Satan sent after Paul.

Demons and Sickness

If you're analytical like me, then you might have taken notice of the last item on the list and thought, "Wait a minute...You said that Paul's thorn in the flesh was NOT a physical problem!"

That's correct. Paul's thorn in the flesh was a demon—not a physical problem. Now, if that demon was *causing* a physical problem, that's fine, as long as we realize that the thorn was a demon and not the problem itself.

On a baseball team, you have a pitcher. A pitcher is not a thrown ball; rather, a pitcher is the person who throws the ball. And in this case, Paul's thorn in the flesh is not a sickness; rather, it is the demon who causes a problem of some kind, which may or may not have been sickness.

This is an important distinction because healing and deliverance are ministered two different ways. When there's no demon at work, it is sufficient to simply tell a crippled person to walk—or ask a blind person, "What do you see?"—or instruct the man with the shriveled hand, "Stretch out your hand." But when a demon is involved, we need to set the captive free before we can instruct them to do something that free people do. In other words, command the demon to leave, and then minister healing.

Demons Like to Return

On at least one occasion, we know that Jesus added something to His command of deliverance:

> **Mark 9:25 –** When Jesus saw that a crowd was running to the scene, he rebuked the impure spirit. "You deaf and mute spirit," he said, "I command you, come out of him **and never enter him again**." (NIV, emphasis added)

That's because demons often return after they've been cast out (whereas sickness and disease, once healed, are done for good).

> **Luke 11:24-26 –** "When an impure spirit comes out of a person, it goes through arid places seeking rest and does not find it. Then it says, 'I will return to the house I left.' When it arrives, it finds the house swept clean and put in order. Then it goes and takes seven other spirits more wicked than itself, and they go in and live there. And the final condition of that person is worse than the first." (NIV)

This difference between demon-induced conditions and purely natural conditions supports our concept of the word "buffet." If Paul's thorn was nothing more than a sickness or other natural condition, then it would have struck him once and then been finished when God brought the victory through healing. But if Paul's thorn was a demon, then it wouldn't matter how many times he told the spirit to

45

leave; it would still occasionally come back to see if Paul would surrender any ground. Even Jesus, after being tempted three times by Satan, had the devil leave only temporarily until "a more opportune time." (See Luke 4:13.)

This repeated returning and repeated attacking—this "buffeting"—would be the sort of thing that Paul would ask God to take away from him. While on one hand Paul had the authority to tell the demon to leave whenever it attacked, he may not have had the authority to tell it never to return. That demon may have been authorized to return from time to time to search for a foothold, which would have reminded Paul to stay humble before the Lord.

Whether the demon was causing a sickness, inciting persecution, or doing one of the other things in the earlier list is not important at this stage. What is important right now is realizing that the word "buffet" makes more sense in the context of Paul's thorn in the flesh being a demon than it being a sickness or disease.

Question 5

Does it Make Sense that Paul would Plead for God to Take Away a Sickness?

O nly one passage in the New Testament uses the term "pray for the sick." (See James 5:14-15.) The rest of the examples we have (in the Gospels and in the book of Acts) involve believers commanding healing in Jesus' name, not asking God to do it.

As it turns out, the problem is not that the Bible contradicts itself; rather, it's that we misunderstand what is meant by "prayer."

Prayer is Not Just Petition

Prayer does indeed involve petitioning God for things

we do not have, but another aspect of prayer is speaking with authority on matters where we have already been granted the authority.

One could say that part of prayer is speaking from earth to heaven while another part of prayer is speaking from heaven to earth. I like to say, though, that the only prayer rightfully uttered from earth to heaven is the prayer of salvation. After that, prayer is spoken from heaven to heaven because we are presently seated with Christ at the right hand of the Father. (See Ephesians 2:6.) So some prayers are offered from heaven to heaven (as we speak to God), and some prayers are offered from heaven to earth (as we speak on God's behalf). After salvation, true, powerful, effective prayer is always offered from our current place with Christ in heaven.

Knowing these two forms of prayer is important. When Jesus taught His disciples how to pray, He directed them to say the phrase that has become classic in King James English: "Thy kingdom come, Thy will be done on earth as it is in heaven." (See Matthew 6:10.) In the original Greek, the implication of the wording is spoken as a command. It could alternately be awkwardly rendered, "Come, Thy kingdom! Be done, Thy will!"

This is not a matter of commanding God, but rather a matter of speaking with authority on matters where God has given us authority. Some of the Lord's Prayer involves asking for things we don't yet have, but this particular line involves speaking with an authority that we do have.

Physical healing is one of the matters where God has instructed us to speak with authority. This is based on the example of Jesus throughout the four Gospels and also the apostles in the book of Acts. Jesus never said, "Ask My Father to heal the sick." Rather, He said, "Heal the sick."

48

(See Matthew 10:8.) It is still God's power that does the work, but it is a measure of God's power that has been distributed to the Christian, along with the authority to wield it. (See Matthew 10:8; Luke 9:1; and Acts 3:6,12,16.)

Praying for Healing: Not What You Think

To "pray" for healing, then, is to speak with authority—not to ask God to do something He has already done. You see, Jesus has already done everything He needed to do in order to put an end to sickness and disease. He paid the price two millennia ago. When Peter quoted Isaiah's prophecy, he changed the tense of the wording from "by His wounds we are healed," to "by His wounds you *have been* healed." (See Isaiah 53:5 and 1 Peter 2:24.) Forgiveness, healing, and deliverance were all purchased at the cross, and there is nothing left for God to do in the matter. As Jesus proclaimed before giving up His life, "It is finished!" (See John 19:30.)

Knowing that "it is finished" is a big deal. It means that there is nothing left for God to do. Accordingly, we do not need to beg for healing. As Randy Clark is noted for saying, "To beg God to heal is to assume you have more mercy than He does." Beyond this, begging God to heal is a misunderstanding of the finished work of Jesus.

Again, Jesus never once told His disciples, "Ask My Father to heal the sick." Rather, He said, "Heal the sick!" (See Matthew 10:8 and Luke 10:9.) Healing is ours to dispense in the name of Jesus through the faith He gives us. (See Acts 3:16.) Jesus told His disciples, "Freely you have received, now freely give." (See Matthew 10:8.)

Praying Before Ministering Healing

It is perfectly acceptable to talk to God in prayer before ministering healing, but not to beg. Prayer of this sort is purely an aligning of the heart with God—perhaps asking for Him to use you or move through you when you speak with authority in His name.

Again, we don't beg for healing; we offer healing in Jesus' name, and Paul knew this. Notice what Paul did on the island of Malta:

> **Acts 28:8-9 –** [The chief official's] father was sick in bed, suffering from fever and dysentery. Paul went in to see him and, **after prayer**, placed his hands on him and healed him. When this had happened, the rest of the sick on the island came and were cured. (NIV, emphasis added)

Notice that it says Paul healed the man, even though we know it was God who did the work. Notice also that it says "after prayer." In other words, the man wasn't healed as Paul begged God for healing. Rather, he was healed when Paul—a man who was intimate with God in prayer—"placed his hands on him and healed him."

Similarly, consider how Paul ministered healing to the man in Lystra:

> **Acts 14:8-10 –** In Lystra there sat a man who was lame. He had been that way from birth and had never walked. He listened to Paul as he was speaking. Paul looked directly at him, saw that he had faith to be healed and called out, "Stand up on your feet!" At that, the man jumped up and began to walk. (NIV)

Again, no begging of God; just a command: "Stand up on your feet!" The same pattern is found throughout the ministry of Jesus and the apostles. You won't find any of them begging God to heal.

(Interestingly, this took place in Lystra—one of the towns of Galatia, where Paul supposedly preached because of an eye problem. If he couldn't see, how did he look directly at the lame man in the crowd? I consider this yet another nail in the coffin of the "eye problem" position.)

No One Begs for What They Already Have

For an apostle who regularly commanded healing with authority to change modes and beg God for his own healing wouldn't make sense. I've commanded my own healing many times and seen immediate results, and I wouldn't call myself greater than the apostle Paul.

If healing was accomplished at the cross, then we don't need to ask for God to heal. There is no sense in asking someone to do something they have already done. And there is no sense begging for something that you already have.

The very nature of healing ministry in New Testament Scripture—including in the life of Paul—eliminates any logical reason for Paul to "beg God" three times to take away a sickness or disease.

If, on the other hand, Paul's thorn in the flesh was a demon, then we can form a logical and Biblically sound case for Paul needing to beg God to keep that spirit away from him (as you will see illustrated later when I explain my own thorn in the flesh). As mentioned, we only know of one case in which Jesus commanded a demon never to return. The rest of the time, demons seem to be authorized to check back from time to time. And for this reason, it is makes sense for Paul to beg God to remove this repeatedly returning spirit once and for all from his life.

Question 6

What Does it Mean for God's Grace to be Sufficient?

Consider the answer that God gave to Paul's pleading (and also Paul's response):

> **2 Corinthians 12:9** – But he said to me, "My grace is sufficient for you, for my power is made perfect in weakness." Therefore I will boast all the more gladly about my weaknesses, so that Christ's power may rest on me. (NIV)

First, Paul begged God three times to take away the demon that was sent to attack him. In response, God made two points: (1) His grace is the answer, and (2) His power is made perfect in Paul's weakness.

Making God's Power Perfect

Let's deal with the second point first. When God said that His power is "made perfect," He didn't mean that His power is somehow imperfect. The Greek term for "make perfect" means "to render a thing full" (*Thayer's Greek Definitions*).

The fullness of God's power is revealed in contrast to weakness, much as the fullness of a light is revealed in contrast to total darkness. If the purpose of God's power is to be more powerful than any other power, then a weak person is the perfect candidate to reveal that power, proving that it is God at work and not the person. (Consider the shepherd-boy, David, defeating the giant warrior, Goliath, in 1 Samuel 17.)

God's Grace is Sufficient

As for the first point, God's grace is a powerful force. Grace is undeserved favor. It is God's expression of goodness toward people who cannot earn His pleasure in their own effort.

Grace is not an emotion; it is an expression of God's nature. So when God said, "My grace is sufficient for you," He didn't mean, "Calm down, Paul! You don't need me to take the demon away; you just need to realize that I like you and let that demon do its thing."

On the contrary, God's grace is active! We are saved by grace, healed by grace, empowered by grace, and transformed by grace. Grace must be expressed for it to truly be grace.

So now we must ask what is meant by the word

"sufficient." This word is translated from the Greek word "*arkeō*," which has an interesting meaning. *Strong's Greek Dictionary* points out that it means "...properly to *ward off*, that is, (by implication) to *avail* (figuratively be *satisfactory*)..." Similarly, *Thayer's Greek Definitions* offer the following thoughts:

> 1) to be possessed of unfailing strength
>> 1a) to be strong, to suffice, to be enough
>>> 1a1) to defend, ward off
> 1b) to be satisfied, to be contented

In the English language, we often use the word "sufficient" in the context of compromise. When we can't have the ideal, we settle for that which is "sufficient." But in the language of the Bible, the word "sufficient" is a word of strength and power. It speaks of the fulfilling of a need. It is a word that properly means to defend against and ward off adversaries, (bringing full contentment).

It is sensible, then, to loosely paraphrase God's answer to Paul as follows: "My grace will defend you and ward off this demon (it will sufficiently meet your need) because you have admitted your weakness and have allowed Me the opportunity to show Myself strong."

This was such an exciting response to Paul that he began to boast about his weaknesses, hoping to remain in the humble position where God's grace and power could continue to "rest on" him. And that's exactly what he did in the following verse:

> **2 Corinthians 12:10** – That is why, for Christ's sake, I delight in weaknesses, in insults, in hardships, in persecutions, in difficulties. For

when I am weak, then I am strong. (NIV)

Question 7
Is it Biblically Sound to Take Pleasure in Sickness and Disease?

Let's recap: Paul begged God to set him free from a demon that Satan had sent to repeatedly attack him (as a reaction to the incredible revelations God had given to Paul). The third time that Paul pleaded for God's help, the Lord responded by granting him a measure of grace that would sufficiently defend him. God's response to Paul's admission of weakness was so powerful and effective that it encouraged Paul to boast all the more in his weakness! He found delight in weaknesses, insults, hardships, persecutions, and difficulties.

It is interesting to note that Paul did not list "sicknesses" or "diseases."

Confusion comes from the use of the word "infirmities" (KJV, NKJV, and AMP) in place of "weaknesses" (NASB, NRSV, ESV, NIV, NLT , RSV, and ASV). While this word can rightly be translated as "infirmities," the context of the passage makes most sense when rendered "weaknesses," which is why most of the popular translations do so—including those recognized as being the most scholarly.

The Greek word used here is the same one used in Romans 8:26, where Paul says, "And the Holy Spirit helps us in our weakness [same Greek word]. For example, we don't know what God wants us to pray for. But the Holy Spirit prays for us with groanings that cannot be expressed in words." (NIV) In this passage, Paul is obviously not talking about sickness or disease, and yet it's the exact same Greek word.

Considering the context of Paul's delight about weakness, it is clear that he's talking about persecution and earthly difficulties, not sickness or disease. (See 2 Corinthians 11:16-33.)

Nobody Brags about Sickness or Disease

If sickness was something to boast about, then why did Jesus constantly heal sicknesses and diseases? If sickness and disease are good things worth bragging about, why would Jesus rob so many people of such a virtuous condition? Was He working against their sanctification? Was He going against the will of the Father?

Jesus never taught people to brag about sickness. He never said to a leper, "Hey, I'm sorry about your condition, but I can't heal you. Turns out you had a prophetic experience fourteen years ago that has rendered you unhealable. You might as well embrace this thing and start bragging to everyone about your leprosy."

Such a speech from Jesus would be utterly unthinkable to those who have studied His life in the Gospels! And yet we seem to have no trouble attributing similar meaning to the words of the Father when He responded to Paul.

Have we forgotten that to see Jesus is to see the Father? (See John 14:9.) Hebrews 1:3 tells us that Jesus "is the radiance of God's glory and the exact representation of his being…" (NIV) If you cannot see Jesus saying something based on the clear revelation of Himself in Scripture, it is sin to assume that the Father would say it. Jesus and the Father are one. (See John 10:30.)

Fix Your Eyes on Jesus

Whenever Jesus encountered sickness and disease, He never praised the condition. Rather, He *always* healed. (See Matthew 4:24; 8:16; 9:35; 12:15; 14:35-36; Mark 6:56; Luke 4:40; 6:18b-19; and Acts 10:38.) And whenever Jesus made a logical case concerning a person's physical condition, He *always* landed on the side of "ought not this person be healed!" (See Mark 3:1-5 and Luke 13:15-16.)

You cannot find a case where Jesus called sickness or disease a virtuous thing. (As a side note, if, in your search for an exception, you're thinking of the man in John 9 who was born blind "for God's glory," remember that Jesus displayed God's glory by healing that man and didn't leave him in his condition!)

F.F. Bosworth writes:

> If Christ's words, "My grace is sufficient," mean
> that He is telling Paul to remain sick, it would be

the first and only instance in the Bible in which
God ever told anyone to keep his disease.
(Bosworth, *Christ the Healer,* Revell, 2007, page
204.)

The Only Favorable Weakness

The question, then, arises as to what kind of weakness
was viewed favorably by Jesus and the apostles? The answer
is found in Paul's list: insults, hardships, persecutions, and
difficulties.

Jesus promised persecution, insults, and difficulty. (See
Mark 10:30; Luke 6:22; John 15:18; and 16:33.) He endured
such things Himself throughout His life and especially when
He went to the cross. From the very moment that the
apostles experienced their first dose of real persecution,
we're told, "The apostles left the Sanhedrin, rejoicing
because they had been counted worthy of suffering disgrace
for the Name." (See Acts 5:41, NIV.)

This is the pattern we see throughout the book of
Acts and even the letters of Paul. Over and over, Paul
boasts about the many times he has been beaten, flogged,
stoned, and so forth. As Paul received persecution (which
proved his weakness against his attackers), God showed
Himself strong through the grace He expressed toward Paul.

In fact, Paul's mention of his thorn in the flesh is
offered right on the heels of a lengthy recounting of the
hardships he has endured. These were his "credentials for
ministry" as he defended his role in God's kingdom against
the many false apostles that were vying for the hearts and
minds of the Corinthian church.

2 Corinthians 11:23-30 – Are they servants of

Christ? (I am out of my mind to talk like this.) I am more. I have worked much harder, been in prison more frequently, been flogged more severely, and been exposed to death again and again. Five times I received from the Jews the forty lashes minus one. Three times I was beaten with rods, once I was pelted with stones, three times I was shipwrecked, I spent a night and a day in the open sea, I have been constantly on the move. I have been in danger from rivers, in danger from bandits, in danger from my fellow Jews, in danger from Gentiles; in danger in the city, in danger in the country, in danger at sea; and in danger from false believers. I have labored and toiled and have often gone without sleep; I have known hunger and thirst and have often gone without food; I have been cold and naked. Besides everything else, I face daily the pressure of my concern for all the churches. Who is weak, and I do not feel weak? Who is led into sin, and I do not inwardly burn? If I must boast, I will boast of the things that show my weakness. (NIV)

Immediately following this discourse comes chapter 12, in which Paul immediately continues his boasting by talking about his heavenly revelation and then quickly bringing the focus back to the hardships he had endured.

This is the context in which we read about Paul's thorn in the flesh. And this is the context in which He says He delights in weakness.

Some Bible scholars believe that Paul's thorn may have been a demon that followed him around and incited riots and persecution wherever he ministered. I do not rule out this possibility, but it is admittedly only a theory.

What's important here is that it is not biblical to boast about sickness or disease. **Every scripture that speaks favorably about suffering—when read in context—has to do with persecution (or the crucifixion of Jesus, which was also persecution), but NEVER sickness or disease.** (See Matthew 16:21; 17:12; Mark 8:31; 9:12; Luke 9:22; 17:25; 22:15; 24:26; Acts 3:18; 5:41; 9:16; 17:3; 26:23; Romans 5:3; 8:17-18; 2 Corinthians 1:5-7; 11:23-33; Ephesians 3:13; Philippians 1:29; 3:10; Colossians 1:24; 1 Thessalonians 1:6; 2:2; 2:14; 2 Thessalonians 1:5; 2 Timothy 1:8; 1:12; 2:3; 2:9; 3:10-12; Hebrews 2:9-10; 2:18; 5:8; 10:32-34; 13:12; James 5:10; 1 Peter 1:6; 1:11; 2:19-23; 3:14-18; 4:1; 4:12-19; 5:1; 5:9-10; Revelation 1:9; and 2:10.) **And in every case where suffering was not viewed favorably, it always had to do with sickness, disease, or calamity; and it usually resulted in healing.** (See Matthew 4:24; 8:6; 15:22; 17:15; Mark 5:26-34; Luke 4:38; 14:2; Acts 7:11; 28:8; 1 Thessalonians 5:9; Jude 1:7; Revelation 2:22; and 9:5.)

Again, to quote F.F. Bosworth concerning Paul's "thorn in the flesh":

> Twenty-five years after he had become an apostle, he wrote to the Corinthians (1 Cor. 11:30), "For this cause many are weak and sickly among you." If Paul's "thorn" was physical infirmity, or he was sick, they would probably write back to him asking, "For what cause are *you* weak and sickly?" (Bosworth, *Christ the Healer,* Revell, 2007, page 205.)

Does God Use Sickness for Good?

There is only one sort of weakness that produces strength in God's kingdom, and sickness isn't it. While we might praise the faith exhibited by a dear friend or loved one who perseveres in loving Jesus despite their physical condition, the fact is that they would be able to do a lot more for Jesus if they were healed and healthy.

God is infinitely wise and knows how to turn any situation around for good. (See Romans 8:28.) So while God is not the author of sickness and disease, He is still fully capable of using the situation until someone on earth has the faith to believe for something different. That's why our character is often shaped in the midst of physical trials, and it's why we can often point to some wonderful lesson learned in the midst of sickness.

But Jesus never told a blind man, "Sorry, bud, My Father is building character in you, so you're going to have to stay blind a while longer." Jesus was clear that "The thief comes only to steal and kill and destroy; I have come that they may have life, and have it to the full." (See John 10:10.) Stealing, killing, and destroying is the work of the devil, not Jesus. And the fact is, Jesus' mission in this world was to destroy the devil's work. (See 1 John 3:8.) That's why He "went around doing good and healing all who were under the power of the devil..." (See Acts 10:38.)

The fact that God can shape us in the midst of sickness does not make sickness a virtuous thing. If that were the case, then Satan would also be virtuous for his ability to be used by God to shape us. Jesus condemned sin at the cross, and the same thing He did to sin, He did to sickness and disease. Jesus would not have purchased healing with His own blood if He knew we were better off sick and diseased.

When we examined the word "buffet" in point four, an interesting Scripture came up:

> **1 Peter 2:19-20** – For it is commendable if someone bears up under the pain of unjust suffering because they are conscious of God. But how is it to your credit if you receive a beating for doing wrong and endure it? But if you suffer for doing good and you endure it, this is commendable before God. (NIV)

If sickness and disease are God's tools for eliminating sin, then such suffering is just. Such a person would be receiving a beating that they deserve. According to Peter, that kind of suffering is not the kind that is "commendable before God." And if that's the case, then we shouldn't delight in it!

If sickness is God's tool for making people into better Christians, then we should all inject ourselves with as many diseases as possible so that we can become more holy. But would this display the power of God? Paul said, "When I am weak, then I am strong," so shouldn't we therefore go out of our way to eat unhealthy food, avoid physical exercise, and catch every sickness and disease we possibly can? Surely we want God's power to be made perfect in our weakness!

I'm sure you see the sarcasm, and it's intended to reveal the underlying ridiculousness of our reasoning when we suggest that God gave Paul a sickness to keep him humble and display His strength. That's not the kind of suffering God promised. The only way God's strength is made perfect in the midst of sickness—the only way He is most fully and truly glorified through it—is when the person is healed. (See John 9:3-7.)

On the other hand, when Christians pass through the fires of persecution, God's power is clearly displayed, and His strength is made known. At no time does Scripture promise sickness or disease to faithful Christians, but it most certainly promises persecution.

> **2 Timothy 3:10-12** — You, however, know all about my teaching, my way of life, my purpose, faith, patience, love, endurance, persecutions, sufferings—what kinds of things happened to me in Antioch, Iconium and Lystra, the persecutions I endured. Yet the Lord rescued me from all of them. In fact, everyone who wants to live a godly life in Christ Jesus will be persecuted. (NIV)

That's the only kind of weakness that brings honor to God, and it is therefore the only kind of weakness worth delighting in. If Paul "delighted in" his thorn, then we must attribute it to this kind of weakness rather than sickness or disease.

Paul was personally weak against the repeated demonic attacks, and he needed God to graciously express divine power on his behalf.

Did Paul Forget to Mention His Sickness to All the Other Churches?

As a final thought on this point, consider the fact that Paul pledged he would "boast all the more gladly" in his weaknesses. (See 2 Corinthians 12:9.) It's interesting to note that Paul is believed to have written about his "thorn in the flesh" (in the book of 2 Corinthians) around 56 AD, and his letter to the Romans was likely written in the same year. The next writings we see from Paul are believed to have started about four or five years later: Philemon was first, then Colossians, Ephesians, Philippians, and then First and Second Timothy.

In these books, we see Paul boasting regularly about persecution. (See Romans 8:35-37; Philemon 1:1; Colossians 1:24-25; 4:2-4,18; Ephesians 3:13; Philippians 1:7,12-14,19-30; 1 Timothy 4:10; 2 Timothy 1:8; 2:9; and 4:6,14-18.) And yet, with all this talk about persecution, we do not see any mention at all about a sickness or disease.

Did Paul forget his promise to "boast all the more gladly" about his sickness? Or could it be that his thorn was no sickness at all?

Obviously, you know where I stand!

Paul did indeed "boast all the more gladly" about his weaknesses! He boasted about the persecutions he had endured, but we do not ever see him boasting about a disease.

This separates the concept of Paul's thorn from the possibility of it being a sickness or disease. If Paul promised to rejoice all the more gladly about sickness, why don't we see any future boasting about sickness? Instead, we see plenty of future boasting about persecution. Similarly, we also see Paul address that our great struggle is not with the physical realm, but rather evil beings in the spiritual realm. (See Ephesians 6:12.) It is clear that Paul knew his thorn was a demon, and it is clear that the only "weakness" he rejoiced in was persecution, hardship, danger, hunger, and other attempts of the demon to "buffet" him.

What was Paul's Thorn in the Flesh?

Paul's thorn in the flesh was a demon. There is no question about this, as Paul himself called it an "angel of Satan." The great controversy remains, though, as to exactly what results this demon was producing in Paul's life.

The fact is, theologians just don't know. Many have speculated all sorts of things, but the truth remains that no one can emphatically say for sure.

In Question 4, I offered a bulleted list of possible ways for a demon to afflict a Christian. Based on that list, here are some Biblically-based possibilities for what Paul's thorn might be:

- Paul's thorn may have been a demon who used others to discourage him in his mission.
- It might have come to regularly tempt Paul
- This demon might have been sent to adversely influence Paul's emotions.
- It may have come to incite others toward violence against Paul.
- Perhaps this demon came to snatch away spiritual seeds that Paul was sowing.
- Maybe all the demon was able to do was to wait for Paul to let his guard down in hopes of outwitting him.
- Maybe this demon was sent to stir others to be an annoyance to Paul.
- It may have been sent to slow down Paul's work for the kingdom of God.
- Perhaps this demon was constantly shoving so-called "Christians" into Paul's path who were only there to cause problems and stir up grief.
- Or that demon could have actually been causing some sort of physical problem in Paul's body.

With all these possibilities, we can certainly narrow the options down to the most likely action of the demon, based on the rest of Paul's writings. If I had to offer my own guess, I would side with the view which seems most prevalent among the leading healing ministers of the last century (like F.F. Bosworth, T.L. Osborn, and many others). The consensus seems to be that the demon came to incite others toward violence against Paul.

This demon was a thorn in Paul's flesh, bringing tremendous aggravation and trouble his way. Paul had apparently begged God three times to take away this demonically-inspired persecution, which was beyond the suffering being endured by the other apostles. Finally, God answered Paul and said that His grace would sufficiently meet Paul's need. He said that His power could be clearly revealed in the midst of Paul's weakness.

So Paul stopped begging God to take away the demon that had been attacking him, and simply pressed on in humility, knowing that God would protect him and keep the enemy from being able to take his life before it's time. Paul continued to faithfully endure persecution, knowing that this demon was limited by God's grace in response to Paul's own admission of weakness and reliance upon God.

Could his "thorn in the flesh" have been any of the other bullet points? Perhaps. But if we are going to draw our conclusion from the whole of Scripture, then the inciting of others toward violence seems the most plausible.

Could someone else experience a "thorn in the flesh" in which a demon is sent by Satan to carry out a different one of those bullet points? Absolutely. In fact, I would like to tell you about my own ongoing struggle with a demon that has been causing a physical problem, and you will see how utterly different this problem is from a typical sickness or disease.

The Story of My Own Thorn in the Flesh

I like to joke that my "thorn in the flesh" is all the people who insist on teaching that Paul's thorn was a sickness! As fun as it is to joke that way, my actual thorn isn't as amusing. It is, however, my joy to share this testimony of God's strength with you, knowing that it will bring an added dose of clarity to this subject.

In 2007, my back went out for the first time. I was unable to walk and was crippled with excruciating pain.

I barely made it to the doctor, who ordered a CAT-scan (rather than the usual MRI since he had the equipment for the CAT scan on-site). The scan revealed two severely bulging discs. I was diagnosed with Degenerative Disc Disease and prescribed strict bed rest with physical therapy twice a week (plus a cocktail of Ibuprofen and Vicodin).

After two weeks, I was finally able to walk—although just barely. My feet barely moved a centimeter at a time. My spine and muscles were in such rough shape that when I tried to stand straight, my torso appeared to be shifted about 3 or 4 inches to the right of my hips. And even then, I couldn't stand or sit for longer than about 15 minutes at a time.

I was a worship leader at a small church-plant in Fowlerville, Michigan, but had missed two weeks due to my condition. On the third week, I begged my parents to drive me there, and I made the painful journey while laying down in the car.

My First Taste of Freedom

During the morning prayer time, I was laying on the floor (as this was the only bearable position for me) when my pastor—on the other side of the room—prayed, "Father, I'm sick of seeing Art hurt like this. Would You please do something?"

Instantly, a series of pops ran up my spine that felt great. I cautiously stood up. Even though I was still feeling a fair amount of pain, my spine was now perfectly straight, and I could walk normally!

I enjoyed sharing the testimony with my physical therapist the next day. She was shocked to see me walk in standing upright and stepping in full strides. The miracle in front of her opened a door for me to pray with her and encourage her to return to the relationship with God that she had admittedly abandoned years earlier.

But I wasn't out of the woods yet. I continued to suffer with Degenerative Disc Disease for four whole years.

I wasn't allowed to lift more than 30 pounds without injuring myself. Between two and four times each year, my back would go out, and I would once again be on strict bed rest with physical therapy. The pain was chronic, and I had to daily take pain medication simply to survive.

During this season, I began working as a youth and children's pastor, married my wife, and experienced the initial revelations of Christ's atonement that launched me into healing ministry in 2009. For almost two years, I ministered healing to countless other people while still struggling with my own bulging and degenerative discs.

The Day I Discovered the Demon

By 2011, I had seen so many people healed that I was convinced God could do anything. And I was convinced through Scripture that it is always God's will to heal. Nevertheless, I was faced with my own condition, which was becoming progressively worse.

In March of that year, my back went out yet again, and I had a small group meeting scheduled at my house in the evening. The closer the time came to the meeting, the more intense my pain became.

That's when I finally realized what was going on.

During my first two years of healing ministry, I learned that if I'm ministering to someone and their pain either moves or intensifies in response to the name of Jesus, then we're dealing with a demon causing the condition. And here I was, with pain intensifying as we neared our small group meeting. I told my wife what was happening and asked her to pray with me.

As soon as we commanded the spirit of infirmity to leave, it was as though someone turned the crank of a vice-grip that was clamped on my spine. The pain went from excruciating to mind-numbing. We continued to command the spirit to leave until suddenly, I felt a release, and could get out of bed.

But this was still only a partial healing. That night, as I was propped up on pillows in a recliner, my small group friends prayed for me and commanded all the pain to leave in Jesus' name. I stood up completely pain-free and began to jump around my living room! It was thrilling!

But by the end of the small group meeting, all the pain had returned. Something wasn't right, but I had never yet encountered anything like this in my limited experience. I could tell I was having a battle with a demon, but I couldn't identify any valid reason for it to keep attacking me.

The Turning Point

A week or two later, in April of 2011, I was at a meeting where I received healing yet again. To make a long story short, after I shared my testimony from the stage, the minister—Will Hart—gave me a prophetic word from the Lord. He said things that only my wife and I had ever talked about, including something that the Holy Spirit had spoken to my wife and me separately the night before. He said that God was calling me into ministry—"not as a pastor at some church, but traveling all over the world," he said. What he didn't know was that three days later was scheduled to be my last Sunday on staff at my church, just before stepping out into fulltime traveling ministry!

This time, the healing stuck. Whereas I wasn't previously allowed to lift more than 30 lbs. (or else my back would go out), I now had no restrictions. Two weeks later, I helped my wife carry a new couch into our house! I was completely healed for the first time in four years.

From Chronic Disease to Buffeting

Since April of 2011, I've been revisited by that same demon several times. The first time was about a month after carrying the couch. I stepped out of my car and could immediately tell that my back was out. "Oh great," I thought, "I wasn't actually healed!" My mind was flooded with fear, and I tried to figure out how I could somehow fall to the grass without injuring myself any further.

That's when something else occurred to me. I call it "Jesus logic." I thought, "Wait a second... I carried a couch!"

I put my hand on my back and said, "Spirit of infirmity, leave in Jesus' name."

Then I stood upright, and was completely fine.

I realized in that moment that the same way demons will try to convince you that you're not saved, they'll also try to convince you that you're not healed. It's all an attack against the same blood of Jesus. It's important to stand in faith for the price Jesus paid and refuse to welcome any lying spirit who would seek to convince you that the healing never occurred.

It was a great lesson, and I've been able to help many other people with what I learned that day. But I soon discovered that I was personally dealing with more than a demon trying to convince me I wasn't healed. I was dealing with a demon who knew I wasn't tricked but still returned from time to time anyway.

The next time that demon came was in October of that year. I was on my first trip to Uganda, ministering in the bush with a Ugandan pastor who lives there. We were scheduled to preach in an all-Muslim village that was overrun with witchdoctors. To reach the village would require a 45-minute motorcycle ride through dirt trails and swampland.

Just before leaving, my back went out.

By this point, I had been healed for about six months and knew it was the same old demon, sent to strike me again. I wasn't intimidated, though. Contrary to conventional wisdom, I mounted the motorcycle and rode to the village. I was in pain the entire time, but it never became worse.

Interestingly, as I preached to the villagers, I didn't have a trace of pain. Forty people were healed, several demons were cast out of people, and fifty people came to salvation. We planted a church in that village that had grown beyond the congregation of fifty by the next time I visited in June the following year.

When the preaching was over, I mounted the motorcycle, and the pain instantly returned until we reached the pastor's home in the other village. Then it left again, and I was back to normal.

Similar things have happened since then, but I have never again been bedridden like I was so many times prior to realizing that a demon was at work. Now, in every case, the demon leaves, and I find myself once again able to carry heavy things, walk normally, and go about life without pain.

I know this demon fits the same category as Paul's thorn in the flesh for several reasons:

- God has given me third-heaven revelations similar to Paul's—things too wonderful for words to express, which could easily stir me toward pride if I'm not kept in check.

- God has called me to a ministry that is physically demanding, so it makes sense for the demon to attack my body.
- The demon regularly returns to "buffet" me—a repeated single blow intended to cause me grief.
- Even though I have authority over the demon, and even though it leaves in every case, I once found myself begging God to keep it from attacking me on such a regular basis.
- God has reminded me to walk in humility so that He can display his strength. Many times, He has shown Himself faithful and warded off this enemy by His grace. The attacks are less and less frequent, and they rarely (if ever) happen when I'm faithfully walking in humility.
- This has encouraged me to be real with people about my weaknesses, my struggles, my difficulties, and the times when this demon comes to strike another blow.

While the demon is not in any way a blessing, I'm encouraged by its presence. I know it means that I have the devil on his toes! He wouldn't send one of his demonic angels after me if I wasn't a threat! Ironically, he keeps winning points for God because every time he manages to land a punch on me, I immediately ask the Lord if I have drifted from humility and readjust my heart accordingly. The demon actually serves to keep me humble before the Lord, which allows the Lord room to demonstrate greater strength!

Based on my personal experience with what I have seen to be a "thorn in the flesh," I completely understand why Paul chose to use this name to describe his experience.

SPIRITUAL TWEEZERS – Art Thomas

What to Do If You Have a Thorn in the Flesh

Speaking as someone who has experienced a "thorn in the flesh" like Paul's, I am convinced that there may indeed be other Christians out there who are encountering the same situation. If that's you, I want to make sure you walk away realizing the good news and practical advice contained in this teaching.

First of all, remember that a "thorn in the flesh"—as Paul used the term—is a demon; not a condition. And the operation of that demon can vary from one person to the next. Whereas for one person, that demon may cause a physical condition, for the next person it may incite others to violence against that believer (remember the list in Question 4). Whatever this demon may be doing, God's promise to you is the same.

God's grace is sufficient for you. In other words, He will fully meet your need—warding off this demon and defending you—as you humble yourself and admit your weakness.

Therefore, boast about your weaknesses. In other words, without complaining, joyfully share the testimonies of hardships and trials that you face. **Remember not to boast, however, about anything Jesus shed His blood to prevent and eliminate.** For example, do not joyfully boast about addictions, bad attitudes, or habitual sins. These are not "thorns in the flesh." Likewise, do not boast about sickness or disease. Jesus paid the price for these as well, and they also are not "thorns in the flesh."

Joyfully boast about the fact that the devil considers you to be a threat. Boast about him sending demons after you, persecutors after you, hardships and trials after you, and for directing insults your way. Rejoice for being counted worthy of suffering for the name of Jesus!

All the while, do not pretend to be strong enough to handle such situations on your own. As you boast about your weakness, remember to technically be boasting about the grace of God that has powerfully defended you.

> **Jeremiah 9:24 –** but let the one who boasts boast about this: that they have the understanding to know me, that I am the Lord, who exercises kindness, justice and righteousness on earth, for in these I delight," declares the Lord. (NIV)

As you do these things, rest in the knowledge that God will continue to graciously protect and defend you.

Hardships will still come from time to time, but you will always come through victoriously! The price Jesus paid is more than enough!

SPIRITUAL TWEEZERS – Art Thomas

What to Do if You Have Realized that Your Condition is NOT a Thorn in the Flesh

Chances are, the vast majority of people who read this teaching will find themselves with the realization that there is not actually a reasonable excuse for them to remain the way they are. That's great news! I hope that this teaching has served to remove all doubt about God's desire to heal you, and now you can move forward in faith and confidence that God wants you to be healed!

Whatever your condition is, it is not a thorn in the flesh. Jesus paid the price for you to be healed. It was the same price He paid for your spiritual salvation. Jesus went to the whipping post so that you could be healed. His body was broken so that yours could be made whole.

Right now, I want to minister healing to you through the written word. I have seen countless people healed through written words, and I believe God wants to do it again for you today!

Whatever your condition is, place your hand in that area if possible. If it's not possible, simply agree with me as we pray.

Do it right now.
Ready?

In Jesus' name, I command every sickness, disease, infirmity, ailment, injury, or any other problem to be completely healed right now.

Be healed in Jesus' name.

Now I want you to test out your condition. Try moving something you couldn't move. Try doing something that you couldn't previously do.

If it was your ears, try listening to some music or asking someone to speak to you. If it was your eyes, try looking with nothing but the eyes God gave you—no glasses. If you couldn't walk, walk in Jesus' name. If you couldn't talk, speak in Jesus' name. If you couldn't bend over, touch your toes in Jesus' name.

Whatever your problem was, do something that can only be done by someone who has been healed of that condition, and praise God for every bit of change!

If you're obviously healed, I want you to share your

testimony with someone as soon as possible. Do it now!

If you only experienced a little change or no change at all, I want you to speak to the condition again with the authority of Jesus' name. Then test it out again. Keep going until you see 100% results.

Conclusion to Part One

Now that you know what Paul's thorn was and why it was given, I hope you can see that it doesn't apply to everyone. Paul didn't write about his thorn so that people everywhere could stay sick. He wrote about his thorn so that the Corinthians wouldn't become distracted by his mention of "abundant revelations." He did it to bring the topic back to his ongoing persecution and hardships (after it had veered uncomfortably into boasting about visions and revelations from the Lord).

So if you ever find yourself preaching or teaching about this passage of Scripture, the focus should be on the suffering Paul endured and the fact that God's grace sustained him and guarded his life. Point out that the "thorn in the flesh" was specifically a demon, and not a sickness or disease. Be clear that Scripture reveals God's will to heal—especially through the life example of Jesus Christ.

I would like to close with the words of F.F. Bosworth:

> Since Paul's "thorn" was no hindrance to *his* faith for the healing of other sick people in the island of Melita, and elsewhere, why should it hinder *ours*? Why *should* it be taught today everywhere as a hindrance to what little faith for healing the sick may have received? The Bible says, "faith *cometh* by hearing," but these days faith *leaves* by hearing—hearing these foolish doctrines. The widespread error concerning Paul's "thorn in the flesh," severs the Gospel. It entirely removes the foundation on which faith for healing must rest. (Bosworth, *Christ the Healer,* Revell, 2007, page 203.)

God wants to heal. Jesus paid the price.

You have been given the responsibility to carry this Good News into all the world.

Will you go?

PART

2

Other Objections to God's Will for Healing

Introduction to Part Two

Paul's thorn is not the only Scriptural case that many like to make against God's will always being healing. In this portion of the book we will examine the following classic objections:

- ❖ Why Isn't Everyone Healed?
- ❖ What about the Pool of Bethesda?
- ❖ What about All the Times God Afflicted People with Disease?
- ❖ What about Job?
- ❖ What about Jacob's Limp?
- ❖ What about Jesus' Hometown?
- ❖ What about King Hezekiah?
- ❖ What about Ananias and Sapphira?

- ❖ What about the Man at the Gate Beautiful?
- ❖ What about Timothy's Frequent Illnesses?
- ❖ What about Paul Leaving Trophimus Sick in Miletus?
- ❖ What about God's Discipline?
- ❖ But Jesus was God!

Some of these have obvious solutions while others may completely shock you. As you'll see, when you look carefully at the scriptures in question, none of these end up being any problem at all.

Many of the objections listed here could be addressed with as much depth as we did Paul's thorn, but I only spent more time there because that seems to be the most common (and most misunderstood) argument out there. My goal in this section is to give you simple answers that you can reference quickly and use whenever someone challenges your belief in God's will to heal.

Some of the solutions in this section are based on principles we've already covered in Part One. So while this section can stand alone as a reference tool, you'll likely receive the most from it if you read Part One first.

Objection 1
Why Isn't Everyone Healed?

As we have already examined in Part One, every person who came to Jesus was healed. You can make a safe biblical case that Jesus didn't heal every sick person He saw (like when He visited the pool of Bethesda and only healed the one lame man, or the likelihood that He may have walked past the crippled man at the temple gate called "Beautiful" who Peter and John later healed in Jesus' name).

The reason for this is best explained in contrast to a question one of my friends asked me. She wondered, "If Jesus came to heal everybody, then why didn't He just snap His fingers and heal everyone on the planet?"

The answer is simple. God is interested in more than healing ministry. His goal is the souls of mankind. If all

Jesus did was heal physical conditions, then everyone would have been physically comfortable for a few decades before spending eternity in hell.

Healing, in itself, was never the point. Healing ministry is a tool, meant to confirm the Gospel of salvation. If Jesus had snapped His fingers and healed everyone, then many would have been healed without any explanation for why they were suddenly feeling better. This would have left the reason up to the people's own imaginations rather than God's grace being revealed through Christ.

The secondary implication of this question is that if it were always God's will to heal, then everyone we pray for would be healed. And yet, experience seems to prove that not everyone we pray for receives healing.

Remember that Scripture tells us that God's will is for no one to perish. (See 2 Peter 3:9.) And yet we know that many people do indeed perish. (See Luke 13:3; Romans 2:12; and 2 Peter 2:12.)

Does the fact that people perish prove that God doesn't want to save everyone? No. God's will is that none should perish. (Again, see 2 Peter 3:9.) In the same way, the fact that not all people are healed does not prove that God doesn't want to heal everyone. Rather, the ministry of Jesus proves the will of God, and Jesus healed everyone who touched Him or called out to Him.

The question of why not everyone is healed is actually a diversion from the greater issue. It is usually asked with the purpose of disproving God's will to heal. But if asked correctly, this question will bring us into a greater demonstration of God's will in the earth.

When the disciples couldn't cast a demon out of an epileptic boy, they later came and asked Jesus why it didn't work. And He told them. (See Mark 9:17-29.)

If we—like the disciples—will begin with the premise that God always wants to heal, it will actually spur us toward solutions rather than accepting everything that happens as being a demonstration of God's providence.

Imagine if we applied that same logic to sin: "Well, I messed up, so obviously it's God's will for me to sin."

Instead, we look for solutions to sin because we know it isn't God's will. We examine ourselves and search for ways to keep ourselves from making the same mistake twice. We allow God to transform and shape us, to renew our minds, and to teach us His ways. As a result, we see greater results in the future.

Isn't that what we want in healing ministry?

Why isn't everyone healed? There may be multiple reasons. But God's will is not one of those reasons. Jesus proved God's will when He paid for it with His blood.

Objection 2
What about the Pool of Bethesda?

An objection I hear fairly often is that at Jerusalem's Pool of Bethesda, many sick people were laying there. But when Jesus came through, He only healed one man and left the rest of them as they were.

Actually, the story of Jesus at the Pool of Bethesda is very useful in making the case for God's will to heal everyone. Let's begin by looking at the passage.

> **John 5:1-8 –** After this there was a feast of the Jews, and Jesus went up to Jerusalem. Now there is in Jerusalem by the Sheep Gate a pool, which is called in Hebrew, Bethesda, having five porches. In these lay a great multitude of sick

people, blind, lame, paralyzed, waiting for the moving of the water. For an angel went down at a certain time into the pool and stirred up the water; then whoever stepped in first, after the stirring of the water, was made well of whatever disease he had. Now a certain man was there who had an infirmity thirty-eight years. When Jesus saw him lying there, and knew that he already had been in that condition a long time, He said to him, "Do you want to be made well?"

The sick man answered Him, "Sir, I have no man to put me into the pool when the water is stirred up; but while I am coming, another steps down before me."

Jesus said to him, "Rise, take up your bed and walk." And immediately the man was made well, took up his bed, and walked. (NKJV)

Why did Jesus only heal the one man and leave the rest alone? There are three simple reasons for this.

First, Jesus didn't heal everyone at the pool of Bethesda because no one called out to Him. Few people actually knew who He was at that point in His ministry. Remember, Jesus didn't heal every sick person He saw, but He did heal every one who touched Him in faith or called out to Him. What made this particular man special was that he had no hope of being healed by the angel (like everyone else there), and his condition had been going on for nearly four decades.

Second, Jesus' visit to the pool was still early in His ministry, and He was arguably trying to "fly under the radar," not wanting to be noticed. This could have been for a couple possible reasons. Perhaps it wasn't His time to become a public figure, and Jesus was still doing all He could to remain hidden until the Father promoted Him. Alternatively, Jesus may have been avoiding the offense that would be produced by Him healing people on the Sabbath. (See John 5:16.) Either case is evidenced by the fact that the man He healed didn't even know who Jesus was because Jesus had slipped quietly back into the crowd after healing him. (See John 5:12-13.)

Third, it's important to remember that even though Jesus was God in the flesh, He was still limited to human form and was therefore "just one guy." It would have taken Jesus all day to minister to the throngs of people by the pool. This is encouraging for any of us who feel guilty walking past someone who has a cast, a crutch, a wheelchair, or some other obvious indication of a need for healing. Like Jesus, we're certainly allowed to approach people whenever compassion moves us; but also like Jesus, we are not under any obligation to heal all the sick people we see. Such activity could be overwhelming.

Another interesting thing to note is that the angel God sent to minister healing at the pool was authorized to heal "whoever" of "whatever." (See John 5:4, NKJV.) In other words, there were no limitations on who was allowed to be miraculously healed when the angel stirred the waters.

Why would God give more authority to an angel than to His own Son? He wouldn't! Jesus too had the authority to heal "whoever" of "whatever" (as we see throughout the rest of His ministry). Those who interpret this Scripture to mean that it's not God's will to heal every person of every disease are actually granting an angel the authority to usurp God's will! If God didn't want to heal just anyone, then He wouldn't give an angel the authority to do so.

Finally, it is great to note how the NIV renders verse

3: "Here a great number of disabled people *used to lie*—the blind, the lame, the paralyzed" (emphasis added). The implication of the Greek language is that these people were no longer there by the time John wrote his Gospel.

I suppose Jesus could have possibly emptied out the pool of Bethesda during His earthly ministry, but this isn't a necessary conclusion. There's another possible explanation: I believe the story in John 5 ends in Acts 5.

In Acts 5:12, we see that all the believers used to meet together in a part of the Temple called Solomon's Colonnade. This covered porch sat just inside the Sheep Gate, and just outside was the Pool of Bethesda.

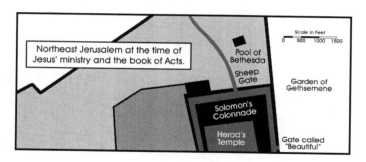

This is where things turn interesting: Just after identifying that the believers were meeting in Solomon's Colonnade in Acts 5:12, Luke continues in verse 16, "Crowds gathered also from the towns around Jerusalem, bringing their sick and those tormented by impure spirits, and *all of them were healed*" (NIV, emphasis added). If the Pool of Bethesda still had anybody laying near it, I have to believe at least one person ran through the Sheep Gate and shouted, "Stop waiting for the angel! Everybody in the Temple Courts is being healed!"

God's will was to heal everyone at the pool.

Objection 3
What about All the Times God Afflicted People with Disease?

God has been known—in both Old and New Testaments—to afflict people with disease from time to time. Before we look at some of these cases, we need to establish something very important about His nature:

> **Lamentations: 3:31-33** – For no one is cast off by the Lord forever. Though He brings grief, He will show compassion, so great is His unfailing love. For **He does not willingly bring affliction or grief to anyone.** (NIV, emphasis added)

If God brings a calamity, it's not His will. He would rather not do such a thing. God's preferred will is always healing and wholeness. If God's will were for people to be sick, then there would be sick people in heaven. But there are not, and we are instructed to pray that God's will would be done on earth just like it is in heaven. (See Matthew 6:10.)

Some of the most dramatic cases of God afflicting people occurred in the Old Testament. Before we look at some of the most notable, we need to consider the purpose and function of the Old Testament (or Old Covenant).

When Jesus came, He ushered in a "New Covenant" of grace, which revealed the true will of God and His nature as a loving Father. Until then, the Old Covenant existed to reveal the problem of sin and confirm the fact that it would result in death. Under the Old Covenant, "The soul who sins shall die." (See Ezekiel 18:20.) But under the New Covenant, "God's kindness, tolerance, and patience" lead us to repentance. (See Romans 2:4.)

Under the Old Covenant, God revealed the power of sin. If it hadn't been for His harsh response to sin during that time, we might never truly understand that "the wages of sin is death." (See Romans 6:23.) And without that understanding, we wouldn't see the power of Christ's victory over sin and death or understand the magnitude of His sacrifice for us. The cross would not have had a context.

It's also helpful to note that while God takes full responsibility for afflicting sinful people, He is not necessarily the One doing the action of afflicting. This is valuable to note because it says something powerful about His nature.

The final straw that allowed for Israel's deliverance from Egypt was the tenth plague, when God promised to kill every firstborn son.

> **Exodus 12:12-13 –** On that same night I will pass through Egypt and strike down every firstborn

of both people and animals, and I will bring
judgment on all the gods of Egypt. I am the Lord.
The blood will be a sign for you on the houses
where you are, and when I see the blood, I will
pass over you. No destructive plague will touch
you when I strike Egypt. (NIV)

But when Moses later explains exactly what is going to
happen, he clarifies, "...He will not permit the destroyer to
enter your houses and strike you down." (See Exodus 12:23.)
In other words, God's actual action during the tenth plague
was to restrain the destroyer and protect His people. He
didn't literally or personally kill the firstborn. "The
destroyer" did that.

But God said that He would strike them down, not
the destroyer. I am convinced that this is because God
regularly takes personal responsibility for the ramifications of
mankind's sin. Of course, the full expression of this
culminates in Jesus' sacrifice on the cross in which God
receives the consequence for our sin fully upon Himself.

So the first thing to note is that just because God says
that He will do something to afflict people doesn't change
His nature as Healer and Protector. In fact, it's most likely
that, while He may have authorized or ordered the affliction,
He was not the one who personally enacted it.

With that foundation laid, let's have a look at some of
the most notable cases where God either afflicted people of
disease or promised to do so.

Deuteronomy 28:15-29 – However, if you do
not obey the Lord your God and do not carefully
follow all His commands and decrees I am giving
you today, all these curses will come on you and

overtake you:

....The Lord will plague you with diseases until He has destroyed you from the land you are entering to possess. The Lord will strike you with wasting disease, with fever and inflammation, with scorching heat and drought, with blight and mildew, which will plague you until you perish....The Lord will afflict you with the boils of Egypt and with tumors, festering sores and the itch, from which you cannot be cured. The Lord will afflict you with madness, blindness and confusion of mind. At midday you will grope about like a blind person in the dark. You will be unsuccessful in everything you do; day after day you will be oppressed and robbed, with no one to rescue you. (NIV, shortened for length)

1 Samuel 5:6-9 – The Lord's hand was heavy on the people of Ashdod and its vicinity; he brought devastation on them and afflicted them with tumors. When the people of Ashdod saw what was happening, they said, "The ark of the god of Israel must not stay here with us, because his hand is heavy on us and on Dagon our god." So they called together all the rulers of the Philistines and asked them, "What shall we do with the ark of the god of Israel?"

They answered, "Have the ark of the god of Israel moved to Gath." So they moved the ark of the God of Israel.

But after they had moved it, the Lord's hand was against that city, throwing it into a great panic. He afflicted the people of the city, both young and old, with an outbreak of tumors. (NIV)

2 Kings 15:5a – The Lord afflicted the king with leprosy until the day he died... (NIV)

2 Chronicles 21:18 – After all this, the Lord afflicted Jehoram with an incurable disease of the bowels. (NIV)

Any time God afflicted someone with disease under the Old Covenant, it was in direct response to their breaking of His righteous laws. Psalm 119:75 says, "I know, Lord, that Your laws are righteous, and that in faithfulness You have afflicted me." The afflictions of God in the Old Testament are seen as expressions of His faithfulness to His righteous laws. Again, this affliction proved the power of sin and gave mankind an understanding of God's righteousness.

But now we live under the New Covenant. Colossians 2:14 says that Jesus "...canceled the written code, with its regulations, that was against us and that stood opposed to us; he took it away, nailing it to the cross." Those who are now in Christ are no longer under the curse of the law. (See Galatians 3:10-14.) Jesus took all the curses of the law upon Himself, and now all that is left for us are the blessings and promises. (See 2 Corinthians 1:20.)

It's therefore easy to answer all the afflictions of the Old Testament by identifying the fact that these people were under a different covenant, and all their afflictions were in direct response to their sin.

Nevertheless, there are two occasions in the New Testament in which it appears God afflicted someone with blindness: First was Saul (on the road to Damascus) and second was the Jewish sorcerer named Bar-Jesus (or Elymas). (See Acts 9:8 and 13:11.) In each case, though, the blindness was only for a time and was not permanent. In Saul's case, Ananias came and ministered healing after only three days; and in Bar-Jesus' case, the blindness was only "for a time" according to Paul's own words. These were both temporary conditions, and they were both special situations in which God stopped an active enemy of the Gospel.

Unless you're actively murdering Christians or going out of your way to hinder or oppose the Gospel, there are no Biblical grounds in the New Testament for God granting you a sickness or disease. And when you look at the ratio of the number of people Jesus healed (everyone who came to Him) compared to the number of people Jesus afflicted (just one: Saul), I don't see any reason to assume that the ratio should be any different today. Jesus is not actively engaged in the afflicting business; He's actively engaged in the salvation business. The thief comes to steal, kill, and destroy, but Jesus came to give abundant life. (See John 10:10.)

The question of whether or not God ever afflicts people with disease is completely separate from the question of whether God always wants to heal. Notice that in the only two New Testament cases of God afflicting people with blindness, the condition was only temporary. This is in line with Lamentations 3:31-33, which was shown at the beginning of this chapter; and that means it was even true in the Old Testament. Even if God afflicts someone, His will is still healing. And when you get right down to it, He probably wasn't the one actively doing the afflicting anyhow.

Objection 4
What about King Hezekiah?

King Hezekiah was the thirteenth king of Judah. He is remembered as a great and good king who destroyed idols, repaired the Temple, reformed the priesthood, and led Israel in a great revival. But despite his righteous reign, he became gravely ill in his late thirties.

Some people use Hezekiah as an argument against God's will to heal because of what the prophet Isaiah said.

> **2 Kings 20:1** – In those days Hezekiah became ill and was at the point of death. The prophet Isaiah son of Amoz went to him and said, "This is what the Lord says: Put your house in order, because you are going to die; you will not recover." (NIV)

If God declared to Hezekiah that he would not recover, then doesn't this prove that it was not God's will to heal him?

But the story doesn't end there. Look at what happens next:

> **2 Kings 20:2-6 –** Hezekiah turned his face to the wall and prayed to the Lord, "Remember, Lord, how I have walked before You faithfully and with wholehearted devotion and have done what is good in Your eyes." And Hezekiah wept bitterly.
>
> Before Isaiah had left the middle court, the word of the Lord came to him: "Go back and tell Hezekiah, the ruler of my people, 'This is what the Lord, the God of your father David, says: I have heard your prayer and seen your tears; I will heal you. On the third day from now you will go up to the temple of the Lord. I will add fifteen years to your life. And I will deliver you and this city from the hand of the king of Assyria. I will defend this city for My sake and for the sake of My servant David.'" (NIV)

Hezekiah's story is actually one of healing! The things we still have to wrestle through, then, are (1) why God would first say that Hezekiah's sickness would definitely result in death when it clearly didn't and (2) why God gave him only fifteen more years, which still sounds like an early death sentence, albeit delayed (Hezekiah died in his early to mid 50's when Psalm 90:10 shows the life expectancy of the time to be around 70-80).

Let's first look at why God would first promise that

Hezekiah's sickness would result in death when, in fact, it didn't. Whether you believe in God's perfect foreknowledge or not, we can all agree that God regularly spoke things within the context of time—often with conditions that depended on mankind's response. But even in the cases where no conditions were listed, the example of Scripture was always that God's proclaimed judgments were up for debate. God declared that He would destroy Israel and start over with Moses, but then relented when Moses prayed. (See Exodus 32:1-14.) Similarly Jonah proclaimed the sure judgment of Nineveh and was later angry that God had relented from the promised judgment in response to the peoples' repentance. (See Jonah 4.) So even though God promised death, His greater will is to answer the prayers of those who seek Him.

Second, we see the problem that God only gave Hezekiah 15 more years. Given the life-expectancy of the time, he arguably could have lived another 20-30 beyond those 15. But God had numbered his days.

I am often confronted by people who accuse me of having a theology in which people never die. "If God always heals people," they argue, "then we would all just live forever!" But who says God needs to use a terrible disease to end a person's life? Why can't He just take them peacefully in their sleep when their time is up? And that does seem to be what happened to Hezekiah, based on the peaceful descriptions of his death. (See 2 Kings 20:21 and 2 Chronicles 32:33.)

In this world, people do die. Every person has an appointment with death. (See Hebrews 9:27.) Solomon taught that there is a time to die. (See Ecclesiastes 3:2.) But he also argues that it's a sad thing for you to "die before your time." (See Ecclesiastes 7:17.)

People do die before their time—otherwise Jesus would not have raised the dead. Interestingly, the dead-raisings we see in Scripture have a common element in that the person is usually identified as having died of a sickness or tragic accident.

It may appear that Hezekiah died at a young age, but the indication of Scripture seems to be that this was his appointed time to die. Fifteen years earlier, when he was deathly sick, was not his appointed time—although it would have happened apart from prayer. People do die before their time, and it's not God's preferred will.

Another apparent problem, which needs to be mentioned, is in Isaiah 38:17. Here Hezekiah prays, "Surely it was for my benefit that I suffered such anguish. In Your love You kept me from the pit of destruction; You have put all my sins behind Your back" (NIV). This verse seems to imply that Hezekiah's illness was God's will for the sake of disciplining him and keeping him from destruction.

While we will examine more of this idea in Objection 12: "What about God's Discipline?" there are two things that need to be noted right now:

First, this was Hezekiah's prayer, not a prophetic word or a teaching. People don't always pray perfect theology. Prayers are expressions of the heart. Hezekiah's prayer may, admittedly, have been a true interpretation of events; but we cannot exalt it above the example Jesus lived. As you'll see in Part Three, Jesus never told someone that they couldn't be healed. He never said, "I'm sorry, but My Father is using this illness for your benefit. It's keeping you from destruction."

Jesus freely healed all. If sickness and disease were such virtuous things meant to make us more like the Lord, then why did Jesus go around robbing everyone of their blessings? Jesus healed everyone, and that tells me that this is not God's preferred method of disciplining His children.

Second, Hezekiah did not have the indwelling Holy Spirit as we believers do today. He was not, therefore, able to rely on the Holy Spirit to produce the fruit of godly character in him. (See Galatians 5:22.) I don't see anything wrong with God using sickness and disease as a character-adjuster in the Old Testament. But as we now live in the New Testament, God lives within us, changes our hearts supernaturally, and produces godly character through us by the inner working of the Holy Spirit. He does not need a sickness to accomplish his will.

There is more to examine with this argument, and we will do so in the response to Objection 12. For now, simply know this: Hezekiah's story is not one of God's reluctance to heal. It is one of God's healing power and a righteous king dying at the correct, appointed time despite his imperfections and mistakes.

God's will is always to heal. In fact, Hezekiah's story teaches us that even when God declares He won't heal a person, He will still change His mind to show mercy if we humble ourselves and pray.

Objection 5
What about Job?

The general objection regarding Job comes from the assumption that everything that happened to Job was God's will. On the contrary, everything that happened to Job was Satan's will.

Not only did Jesus distinguish between the stealing, killing, and destroying of "the thief" and His own mission to give abundant life (in John 10:10), but James gave us a similar contrast that directly relates to Job's story:

> **James 5:11** – As you know, we count as blessed those who have persevered. You have heard of Job's perseverance and have seen what the Lord finally brought about. The Lord is full of compassion and mercy. (NIV)

Job is praised for his endurance in the midst of all the evil that befell him, and God is praised for the end result in which Job received double of everything that was taken from him and one-hundred-forty years of long-life to enjoy it!

Read the book of Job carefully. All the terrible things that happened to Job were done by Satan. James is clear that Job should be commended for persevering during Satan's attack. He is also clear that God's action didn't happen until after the attack (which is why he uses the word "finally"). "The Lord is full of compassion and mercy," but there was nothing compassionate nor merciful about what happened to Job. The afflictions were not God's work; they were Satan's.

It is dangerous to look at all the wrong that happened to Job and attribute it to God.

Job 1:22 – "In all this, Job did not sin by charging God with wrongdoing."

Scripture says it is sin to claim that Job's suffering was enacted by God. Verses 6-12 of Chapter 1 are clear that the "wrongdoing" against Job was committed by Satan. It's true that God lifted the "hedge of protection" around Job, which allowed Satan access to his possessions and family, but He's not the one who did the afflicting.

Some have suggested that God "picked on" Job by bringing the devil's attention to him. Here is what the passage says:

Job 1:6-12 – One day the angels came to present themselves before the Lord, and Satan also came with them. The Lord said to Satan, "Where have you come from?"

Satan answered the Lord, "From roaming throughout the earth, going back and forth on it."

Then the Lord said to Satan, "Have you considered my servant Job? There is no one on earth like him; he is blameless and upright, a man who fears God and shuns evil."

"Does Job fear God for nothing?" Satan replied. "Have you not put a hedge around him and his household and everything he has? You have blessed the work of his hands, so that his flocks and herds are spread throughout the land. But now stretch out your hand and strike everything he has, and he will surely curse you to your face."

The Lord said to Satan, "Very well, then, everything he has is in your power, but on the man himself do not lay a finger."

Then Satan went out from the presence of the Lord. (NIV)

At first blush, it does look like God thought, *Hmm... It seems Satan is having trouble finding someone to attack. Maybe I'll pick someone for him to destroy.* But to interpret the passage this way would be inconsistent with everything we know about God's nature—especially as it is revealed through Jesus. (See Hebrews 1:3.)

It makes much more sense to me if we interpret the dialogue more like this:

"Satan; what are you doing here?"

"I was roaming throughout the earth, looking for someone to devour, and I'm exhausted. I can't seem to find anyone."

"I know. Isn't it great? Have a look at my servant Job. You can't even lay a finger on him!"

"Of course he's living a righteous life; You're making everything go well for him. If it weren't for Your protection and blessing on his life, he would be a much different person. I bet if you attacked him even a little, he would curse You to Your face."

"You clearly don't know My servant Job. Go ahead and attack his possessions, but leave him alive, and I assure you that he will put you in your place."

When reading the passage through this lens, we see a God who has confidence in His servant. It would be one thing for God to directly oppose Satan; but whenever God allows human beings the privilege of opposing the devil, it reveals the devil's fallen condition even clearer. God knew Job would be victorious over the wrongdoing of the devil and blessed him with the opportunity to experience that victory. And all this served to remind the devil of his powerlessness against the people of God.

Satan's action in the life of Job was to strip him of everything he had. God's action in the life of Job was to bless him in the end with double of everything the devil stole from him. (See Job 42:10.) The "wrongdoing" was the devil's action. God's action was to overcompensate with a double blessing.

As a final thought, Job (being an Old Testament figure) didn't have the authority to speak in Jesus' name. Accordingly, he couldn't command the devil to leave. We, on the other hand, have been granted the authority to "overcome all the power of the enemy," and this came with the promise that "nothing will harm you." (See Luke 10:19.) To say that God could allow Satan to attack us (in a way that we would be powerless against it) would be to call Jesus a liar. Jesus said nothing would harm me because I have authority over all the power of the devil. "…The one who is in you is greater than the one who is in the world." (See 1 John 4:4.) Our faith in Jesus provides us with protection against every single attack of the enemy. (See Ephesians 6:16.)

Based on the teachings of Jesus, the examples in the book of Acts, and the sound doctrine of New Testament Scripture, there is no sensible way to suggest that any Spirit-filled Christian could possibly experience the same situation as Job did and not have the authority to command the devil to leave.

Objection 6
What about Jacob's Limp?

I can't tell you how many people I have heard argue that Jacob's limp justifies their sickness or disease. "Well," they say, "Jacob did limp for the rest of his life, and it was a good thing that God did. So maybe this is something like that."

I sharply disagree; and in a moment, you'll see why.

In Genesis 32:22-32, we read the account of the patriarch, Jacob as he wrestled with God in a human form. Jacob insisted on receiving a blessing, and he received one; but not until "the man" (actually God) somehow touched the tendon in the socket of his hip, causing Jacob to limp. (See Genesis 32:25 and 31-32.)

Our pulpits, our bookstores, and the Internet are full

of teachings, books, and articles that mention Jacob's limp. And—in my experience—the most common statement about that limp that you'll hear and read is that "Jacob limped for the rest of his life."

Strangely, that's not found anywhere in the Bible.

The closest thing we have to it is a single moment when Jacob (a.k.a. "Israel") "leaned on his staff." Here are the two accounts:

> **Hebrews 11:21 –** By faith Jacob, when he was dying, blessed each of Joseph's sons, and worshiped as he leaned on the top of his staff. (NIV)

> **Genesis 47:28-31 –** Jacob lived in Egypt seventeen years, and the years of his life were a hundred and forty-seven. When the time drew near for Israel to die, he called for his son Joseph and said to him, "If I have found favor in your eyes, put your hand under my thigh and promise that you will show me kindness and faithfulness. Do not bury me in Egypt, but when I rest with my fathers, carry me out of Egypt and bury me where they are buried."

> "I will do as you say," he said.

> "Swear to me," he said. Then Joseph swore to him, and Israel worshiped as he leaned on the top of his staff. (NIV)

Some have assumed that the detail of Jacob "leaning on his staff" implies that he still had a limp. In context, though, he was an old man at this time (a hundred and forty-seven years old), he was near to death, and he may have only leaned on his staff because he was so frail.

When we read about Moses, Aaron, Elisha, and others carrying a staff, we never draw the assumption that they needed such a tool due to having a limp. We only draw that conclusion about Jacob because of the experience he had when he wrestled with God.

If you were to remove the story of Jacob wrestling with God, no one would think twice about a one hundred and forty-seven year old man leaning on a staff while he worshipped God. No one would assume that it was because he had a limp; rather, they would be perfectly comfortable acknowledging that he was an elderly man who was close to death. It probably took a lot for him to stand at that point!

Actually, we see Jacob being very physically active—even immediately following his divine encounter. He bowed seven times before Esau—something that would be difficult for someone whose hip was dislocated; and it says that he did this "on the way" to his brother, which implies that he may have stood back up to his feet, walked a bit, and bowed again each time. (See Genesis 33:3.) He built a house for himself and shelters for his animals. (See Genesis 33:17.) He camped. (See Genesis 33:18-19.) He traveled. (See Genesis 35:1-7; 46:1-7.) He also built a few altars and stone memorials in the years following his encounter. (See Genesis 33:20; 35:7,14, and 20.) That's a lot of strenuous physical activity for someone whose hip is out of socket!

So to say that "Jacob limped for the rest of his life (and therefore I should have my sickness or disease for the rest of my life)" is a very weak argument and impossible to prove. The Bible doesn't actually say any such thing. All it says is that Jacob limped when the sun was rising above him immediately after his encounter with God. (See Genesis 32:31.) That's a very specific, time-sensitive verse; and we never hear the word "limp" associated with Jacob ever again.

In fact, as if to challenge the traditional view even further, it's interesting to note that the Hebrew word translated "limp" (in the NIV and other versions) is only used seven times in the Bible (*tsela'*). One of those times refers to Jacob. Three of those times could arguably be translated to imply "a lame person" or "one who stumbles." And the other three times, it is very clearly used to refer to a one-time "stumble" rather than an ongoing limp. Here are those three cases:

> **Psalm 35:15 –** But when I stumbled [*tsela'*], they gathered in glee; assailants gathered against me without my knowledge... (NIV)

> **Psalm 38:17 –** For I am about to fall [*tsela'*], and my pain is ever with me. (NIV)

> **Jeremiah 20:10 –** ...All my friends are waiting for me to slip [*tsela'*]... (NIV)

In all three cases, the word "limp" would not make any sense. Instead, the word is translated as "stumble," "fall," or "slip." It would therefore be perfectly sensible to translate Genesis 32:31 to say, "The sun rose above him as he passed Peniel, and he [stumbled] because of his hip." (See NIV, alternate translation mine.)

The other three Scriptures that use the word *"tsela'"* use it to describe a person rather than referring to an action. When the word is used to describe a person, it is translated in the NIV as "lame." (See Micah 4:6, 4:7, and Zephaniah 3:19.) In context, this translation fits. But whenever the word is used to define an action rather than a person, it usually refers to a single act of stumbling rather than an ongoing condition. In the case of Jacob's so-called "limp," the word is used to describe an action rather than a person. It is used as a verb rather than as an adjective.

It therefore becomes entirely plausible that Jacob didn't limp at all but rather only stumbled once because of his hip. Whatever the case, whether he limped or stumbled while the sun rose on him at Peniel, we have already seen that it is highly unlikely that this was a life-long condition.

All this aside, what if Jacob did indeed limp for the rest of his life? Does that validate chronic illness?

I like to say, "If you can honestly tell me that you received your cancer (or whatever disease) while physically wrestling God in human form, then feel free to stay sick. If not, then why are you trying so hard to remain sick and keep Jesus from receiving what He paid for?"

If Jacob limped for the rest of his life, it would not validate someone else having a sickness or disease for the rest of their lives. For one thing, his limp was not a sickness or disease; it was an injury. It could possibly, then, validate physical injury, except that this injury was specifically received from a physical confrontation with God in bodily form. If your injury came any other way, then don't apply this scripture to your condition.

Saul (later Paul) was left blind after his own encounter with Jesus, but it only lasted three days before he was healed. (See Acts 9:9.) The fact that Paul was blinded after an encounter with God doesn't mean he was blinded for the rest of his life. And the fact that Jacob limped (or, more likely, stumbled) after an encounter with God doesn't mean that he limped or stumbled for the rest of his life.

"Jacob's limp" (or "stumble") is a weak argument against healing, and it simply doesn't apply when you study the Scriptures.

Objection 7
What about Jesus' Hometown?

When Jesus visited His hometown of Nazareth, the Gospel writers tell us that He ran into a problem.

Mark 6:1-6 – Jesus left there and went to his hometown, accompanied by his disciples. When the Sabbath came, he began to teach in the synagogue, and many who heard him were amazed.

"Where did this man get these things?" they asked. "What's this wisdom that has been given him? What are these remarkable miracles he is performing? Isn't this the carpenter? Isn't this Mary's son and the brother of James, Joseph, Judas and Simon? Aren't his sisters here

> with us?" And they took offense at him.
>
> Jesus said to them, "A prophet is not without honor except in his own town, among his relatives and in his own home." He could not do any miracles there, except lay his hands on a few sick people and heal them. He was amazed at their lack of faith. (NIV)

The way I typically hear this passage interpreted suggests that Jesus' ability to heal was somehow suppressed or diminished because of the unbelief of the people around Him. Since the people didn't have faith, Jesus was limited to only healing a few sick people. Their lack of faith overpowered whatever faith He had, and He found Himself firing blanks.

If you try to write a screenplay of this scene, you run into some problems with this interpretation. Here we have Jesus with His hands on a blind man. He commands the man's eyes to open, but nothing happens. He tries again, but nothing happens. He tries again, and still nothing happens. Finally, our exasperated Lord turns to the onlookers and declares, "Come on, people! You need to believe more! You're keeping this man blind!"

That's not the Jesus I know.

In reality, the answer is much simpler. Let me ask you a question: Why is it that you don't ask the clerk at a gas station to heal you? Why is it that you don't ask the waiter at a restaurant to heal you? Why is it that you don't ask your local carpenter to heal you? The answer is simple: he's just a carpenter. He doesn't have anything to offer.

The people murmured among themselves: "Isn't this the carpenter? Didn't he grow up here? He's no Messiah! What does he have to offer?"

Jesus identified that the people's problem was not that they didn't believe in miracles—it was that they didn't honor Him as a prophet. The indictment of verse six wasn't against their belief in God; it was about their lack of trust in Jesus the minister. They didn't think He had anything to offer. And it makes the most sense that Jesus couldn't do many miracles there because the people—who didn't believe He had anything for them—didn't even go to Him. Again, would you ask your local carpenter to lay hands on your sick child?

We tend to treat faith like a force when it's actually the opposite. Faith is restful trust. Faith is ceasing from unnecessary effort and actively depending on someone else's effort. I express my faith in my wife by not hovering over her shoulder as she cares for my children or constantly checking in to make sure they're safe. My wife is trustworthy, and my action of restful trust proves my faith in her ability to care for my children. Faith in God is similar—we do only what we are asked to do and completely trust Him to do the rest on our behalf.

But when it comes to healing ministry during the life of Jesus, the question was never really about the people's faith in God. If the key component was the person's perfect faith in God, then they wouldn't have needed to touch Jesus. They would have been healed all alone apart from Him. They people didn't know that Jesus was God. At best, some thought of Him as the Messiah, but that didn't necessarily mean divinity in their minds. Most just called Him "teacher" or "rabbi." So whenever Jesus said, "Your faith has healed you," He was pointing out their faith in him as a healing minister. These people believed and trusted that if they could only touch Jesus—the man—they would be healed.

Jesus explained the lack of faith in His hometown as a

lack of honor for His ministry. The people didn't expect anything from Him, and only a few sick people went to him for healing (or perhaps were just too weak to walk away).

But there's another interesting component to the story. In Luke's account of Jesus in His hometown, we read this:

> **Luke 4:22-24 and 28-30 –** All spoke well of him and were amazed at the gracious words that came from his lips. "Isn't this Joseph's son?" they asked.
>
> Jesus said to them, "Surely you will quote this proverb to me: 'Physician, heal yourself!' And you will tell me, 'Do here in your hometown what we have heard that you did in Capernaum.'"
>
> "Truly I tell you," he continued, "no prophet is accepted in his hometown..."
>
> All the people in the synagogue were furious when they heard this. They got up, drove him out of the town, and took him to the brow of the hill on which the town was built, in order to throw him off the cliff. But he walked right through the crowd and went on his way. (NIV)

The people sure didn't leave much time for healing ministry!

Because of their lack of faith in Jesus, the people rejected Him. They didn't flock to Him for healing as they did in other towns. Instead, those who flocked to Him only did so to kill Him!

If Jesus' ability to heal was somehow mystically

impeded by unbelief in the hearts of people, then how did Jesus heal the epileptic boy when He identified everyone around Him as an "unbelieving and perverse generation?" (See Matthew 17:17.) Even His own disciples didn't have faith for the boy to be healed! (See Matthew 17:20.)

This is not a Scripture about the magical power of unbelief. It's a passage about what we see in people. If we can't see that a person represents God, we won't go to them for healing ministry. Even today, as every Christian is part of the Body of Christ, we need to recognize them as such. You don't need to chase down faith healers; just touch the hem of someone's garment at church! Stop looking at the earthly identity of the Christians around you, and start looking at their heavenly identity. Those people are the body of Jesus in this world. Many Christians are sick and even dead because they failed to discern that Jesus body was within reach and that He was fully capable of healing them through the ordinary Christians all around them. (See 1 Corinthians 11:29-31.)

I find it funny whenever people bring up this passage as an argument against God's will to heal. Even if they misinterpret the passage and assume that Jesus' healing power was overcome by a cloud of unbelief, they have to admit that the miracles would have happened if the people had believed. In other words, the problem wasn't with God's will; it was with the hearts of the people. In this passage, God still wanted to heal everyone.

God's will was for Nazareth to be healed, but the will of the people was to reject Jesus and throw Him off a cliff.

SPIRITUAL TWEEZERS – Art Thomas

Objection 8
What about Ananias and Sapphira?

During the early days of the Church, people regularly sold pieces of land and brought the money to the apostles. These finances helped them focus their working hours on ministry, feed hungry widows, and likely more.

But one couple—Ananias and his wife, Sapphira—engaged in an unfortunate deception. They sold their land and claimed to lay all the money from the sale at the feet of the apostles, but the truth is that they withheld some.

Ananias and Sapphira's sin was not that they withheld some money from the sale of their land. Their sin was that they lied about it and claimed to give everything. While we can only speculate about their intentions, a cursory look at sinful human nature tells us that they probably wanted to have the reputation of generosity (being more concerned about the thoughts of people than the thoughts of God) while still enjoying the riches of this world. Whatever the case, they lied, and it came back to bite them.

> **Acts 5:1-11** – Now a man named Ananias, together with his wife Sapphira, also sold a piece of property. With his wife's full knowledge he kept back part of the money for himself, but brought the rest and put it at the apostles' feet.
>
> Then Peter said, "Ananias, how is it that Satan has so filled your heart that you have lied to the Holy Spirit and have kept for yourself some of the money you received for the land? Didn't it belong to you before it was sold? And after it was sold, wasn't the money at your disposal? What made you think of doing such a thing? You have not lied just to human beings but to God."
>
> When Ananias heard this, he fell down and died. And great fear seized all who heard what had happened. Then some young men came forward, wrapped up his body, and carried him out and buried him.
>
> About three hours later his wife came in, not knowing what had happened. Peter asked her, "Tell me, is this the price you and Ananias got for the land?"
>
> "Yes," she said, "that is the price."
>
> Peter said to her, "How could you conspire to test the Spirit of the Lord? Listen! The feet of the men who buried your husband are at the door, and they will carry you out also."

> At that moment she fell down at his feet
> and died. Then the young men came in and,
> finding her dead, carried her out and buried her
> beside her husband. Great fear seized the whole
> church and all who heard about these events.
> (NIV)

If God's will is always to heal, then why did He kill Ananias and Sapphira? Why wasn't it sufficient to simply rebuke them and carry on?

Admittedly, this is probably the most difficult objection to work with—not because there isn't an answer, but because it isn't a comfortable one.

I am aware of teachers out there who blame this couple's death on Peter mishandling the situation, suggesting that his words were what killed them, not God. But I can't reconcile that view with the rest of Scripture. I'm also aware of people who suggest that the text doesn't actually say God killed them, and maybe it was just the stress of being confronted by the lead apostle. But it seems to me that in such a case, Peter would have raised them from the dead. I've probably read every explanation that removes their death from any association with the will of God, but I can't comfortably embrace any of those views without compromising something else or being intellectually inconsistent.

This may surprise you, but I don't actually have a problem with an interpretation in which God ended Ananias and Sapphira's lives (though remember from Objection 3 that while He may have taken responsibility, the act itself was likely carried out by an angel, as when God ordered Herod's death in Acts 12:23).

Since there's not a lot to work with in this text to form

133

an absolute, undeniable conclusion, the best I can do is offer my best understanding based on what I know of God from the rest of Scripture.

The first thing to note is that God knew whether or not Ananias and Sapphira had any chance of repenting. If there was any inkling of a chance, He wouldn't have ordered their deaths. God doesn't want anyone to perish in hell. (See 2 Peter 3:9.) This is bad news for Ananias and Sapphira, but great news for every other person in the world. As long as you're still breathing, God believes there is hope for you! Choose Him today before it's too late!

The second thing to note is that God is a loving Father who has been known to make examples of people so that He can have mercy on future generations and give them more time to repent. Read what Paul wrote to the Corinthian believers:

> **1 Corinthians 10:1-12 –** For I do not want you to be ignorant of the fact, brothers and sisters, that our ancestors were all under the cloud and that they all passed through the sea. They were all baptized into Moses in the cloud and in the sea. They all ate the same spiritual food and drank the same spiritual drink; for they drank from the spiritual rock that accompanied them, and that rock was Christ. Nevertheless, God was not pleased with most of them; their bodies were scattered in the wilderness.
>
> Now these things occurred as examples to keep us from setting our hearts on evil things as they did. Do not be idolaters, as some of them were; as it is written: "The people sat down to eat and drink and got up to indulge in revelry."

We should not commit sexual immorality, as some of them did—and in one day twenty-three thousand of them died. We should not test Christ, as some of them did—and were killed by snakes. And do not grumble, as some of them did—and were killed by the destroying angel.

These things happened to them as examples and were written down as warnings for us, on whom the culmination of the ages has come. So, if you think you are standing firm, be careful that you don't fall! (NIV, emphasis added)

God's judgments against sin in the Old Testament happened as examples to us. And He ensured that these things were written down so that we would be warned and have a healthy fear of sin's power despite the mercy and liberty He continues to pour out by His grace. By having people write down the judgments of the past, God's hope is that He won't have to do such a thing again to prove His desire for holiness but that we will simply read the example and take Him seriously based on the testimony alone.

Interestingly, that's exactly what happened when Ananias and Sapphira died. Acts 5:11 says, "Great fear seized the whole church and all who heard about these events."

While this passage is not technically about sickness or healing, it does teach us something about God's nature. God is not in the business of killing people whenever they lie to a minister of the Gospel. If that were the case, there would be a whole lot more dead people in our churches today! God only had to take such harsh action once, and then He inspired Luke to write it down so that future generations could learn not to lie to the Holy Spirit. Such a sin is very serious and shouldn't be taken lightly.

God's swift and serious consequence against Ananias and Sapphira was actually an expression of His mercy toward future generations. He did it for our sake so that we could have more time to repent. In the grand scheme of things, the untimely death of two people who weren't likely to repent is nothing in comparison to the lesson we learn about the holiness of our New Testament God and His fiery desire for honesty and integrity throughout the Church.

Objection 9

What about the Man at the Temple Gate "Beautiful"?

Early in the life of the New Testament Church, we see Peter and John on their way into the Temple to pray around three in the afternoon. As they came to the Temple gate called "Beautiful," a crippled beggar called out to them for money.

According to Acts 3:2, this man was carried there every day. Many have suggested that this is a problem because it's very likely that Jesus walked through this same Temple Gate during His ministry, and the man was never healed.

I want to get something really obvious out of the way: In the account recorded in Acts 3, the crippled man was healed. So we know it was God's will to heal him! The question posed through this story is about why (if it was God's will) Jesus didn't heal the man sooner. Could it be that it wasn't God's timing? And if it wasn't God's timing, then could it be that there are people today who God doesn't want to heal until a better time?

This entire question is based on a speculation that Jesus walked past this man during His earthly ministry. I'm sure Jesus walked passed a lot of sick people. The Pool of Bethesda is another example, which we have already addressed. I could simply leave the response at that, but it's worth adding that there is actually a reasonable case to be made that the two may never even have crossed paths.

For one thing, The Gate Beautiful isn't the only entrance into Jerusalem. The big, walled city had ten gates. So first, we have to establish that in a sense, there was only a one-in-ten chance that Jesus regularly used that particular gate (actually a little higher of a chance since it was the gate with the most direct access to the Temple from outside the city, but there were still nine other options that need to be considered).

Second, we need to recognize that the time of day was a factor. In the Acts 3 account, verse 1 says that it was 3:00 in the afternoon, and verse 2 says that the man was only then being carried to his usual begging spot. In other words, if this was the man's normal time of arrival, then he was only there for a few hours a day—probably from about 3:00 until supper time (or perhaps sooner). So even if Jesus did use that gate, if He used it anytime during the first half of the day or anytime after the beggar went home (like after dinner), the beggar wouldn't have been there. This cuts whatever chances of their paths crossing at least in half.

Third, Jesus didn't live every day in Jerusalem. In fact,

John records Him only going there three times during His ministry. (See John 2:13; 5:1; and 12:12.) In the first two passages, Jesus came to Jerusalem from Capernaum and Galilee. This would have had Jesus coming from the north or northeast, making the Gate Beautiful an unlikely entrance or exit for His journey. Nevertheless, even if He did use that gate, the text of Acts 3 does not indicate or require us to accept that the crippled man had been visiting this spot for years—it's entirely possible he had only been there a few months.

Only in the third passage did Jesus definitely approach Jerusalem from the east—specifically, the nearby village of Bethany. And only at this time—mere months before Acts 3—do we have reason to assume that the crippled man might have already been camping out at the gate. When traveling from Bethany, the road splits four ways, allowing the traveler to choose any of four gates along the eastern wall of Jerusalem. It seems to me that the Gate Beautiful was the most likely entrance on this occasion (Matthew 21, Mark 11, and Luke 19 all seem to imply that Jesus entered directly into the Temple courts), but He did so riding on a donkey—it was the Triumphal Entry. Jesus passed through that gate in the midst of pandemonium as throngs of people shouted "Hosanna!" and waved palm branches.

Mark 11:11 seems to imply that it was already late when Jesus arrived, so He only visited the Temple briefly before going back to Bethany. Since it was late, it's possible that the lame man had already been carried home by then. But even if he was there, the festival crowd shouting "Hosanna" and pressing around Jesus wouldn't really make one-on-one time with the crippled man an easy task. And on His way out, the wild commotion caused when Jesus turned over tables and rebuked the money changers probably wasn't the best setting to pause and minister healing either.

Now, Luke 19:47 tells us that at this time (during the week-long Passover feast), Jesus was teaching "every day" in the Temple. If we assume that He was staying in Bethany, then this does likely bring Him through that gate a few more times on Monday through Thursday of that week. But again, we have to consider that He could have used one of four gates each time (and He may have changed it up a couple times since He occasionally liked to avoid the waiting crowds).

We also have to consider the time of day that He likely passed through that gate. Personally, I would expect Him to teach during the mornings—not as an interruption or a distraction during the three o'clock time of prayer (which is when that crippled beggar seems to regularly come). So the main time of day Jesus used that gate would not have been the time of day when the beggar was there.

But there's one more thing to consider: While modern readers might think that this influx of pilgrims was the most ideal time for a beggar to make some extra money, an understanding of the culture would suggest that the man may have been with his family or friends (whoever carried him to the gate every day) and celebrating the weeklong Feast of Unleavened Bread with them. For one thing, if I were a crippled beggar, I wouldn't pass up a feast; but more importantly, this feast was an act of worship to honor God, and all Israel was commanded and expected to participate.

In short, while not impossible, the chances are reasonably low that Jesus and the crippled beggar ever even crossed paths.

The people who use this argument make it sound like Jesus passed this man every single day for multiple years. But the truth is that Jesus may never have seen him at all.

140

Nevertheless, even though I just spent a lot of time explaining why Jesus might never have seen the man, the fact is that the argument doesn't hinge on this disputable point. The clincher is this: Even if Jesus did walk by the man before, it is just a further reminder that Jesus didn't heal every single person He saw. Such a task would have been overwhelming. I walk past sick people too, and I believe God wants to heal them all. It's just not practical to stop for every single unsuspecting person.

If you ask me, the real question is this: With all the miracles being reported all over Jerusalem, why did no one ever bring this man to Jesus for healing? Could we possibly be looking at another case where someone didn't trust that Jesus could deliver healing and therefore never even approached Him?

This man's healing wasn't a matter of God's timing. Peter and John didn't decide to stop because the Holy Spirit had somehow communicated that it was time for them to go find the man—rather, they stopped because the man called out to them and initiated the conversation. It is entirely possible that this was the first time this man actually engaged one of God's agents of healing (a fair guess considering the high level of healing results recorded during these early days of the Church).

Finally, when Peter and John were questioned about the healing, they didn't give credit to God's timing—they gave credit to Jesus' name and the faith that comes through Him. (See Acts 3:16.)

"Now is the day of salvation."

Objection 10

What about Timothy's Frequent Illnesses?

Timothy was a child of God and a Church leader who suffered from stomach problems and frequent illnesses. Paul gave him this advice:

> **1 Timothy 5:23** – Stop drinking only water, and use a little wine because of your stomach and your frequent illnesses. (NIV)

Some have used Paul's advice to Timothy as a way of saying that it wasn't God's will to heal him. This argument is based on the assumption that if God wanted to heal Timothy, then he wouldn't need any sort of medicinal wine.

I, however, preach and demonstrate a different sort of healing ministry. While I believe that Jesus healed every person who came to Him, and while I believe that He always did it within the day (rather than over a long period of time), I do not have a problem with the possibility of my faith not being exactly like the faith of Jesus.

For this reason, I recognize that some conditions require perseverance on my part as a healing minister. This isn't because God doesn't want to heal the person—if Jesus touched the person, then they would be healed by now! On the contrary, it's because my faith hasn't yet reached the level of Jesus' faith.

I've seen some pretty dramatic miracles. As I'm writing, in the last month, I've seen God instantly and miraculously heal fibromyalgia, neuropathy, broken bones, dislocated bones, bone spurs, deaf ears, diabetes, arthritis, back injuries, and pains of all sorts. But there were still a handful of people to whom I ministered who were not healed. My advice to them was that they continue seeing their doctors and continue seeking God for healing.

Based on my personal experience in healing ministry, it is not a reflection on God's will if I encourage someone to seek medical relief from their condition. Rather, it is an act of compassion toward the person, encouraging them that it's okay to have medicinal relief from their symptoms while they continue to seek the healing Jesus paid for.

Paul did not give Timothy this advice because God didn't want to heal Timothy. In fact, if sickness is God's will, then it's actually sinful to take medication! If God wants you to be in pain, then to take pain medication is to go against God's will! If God wants you to have high blood pressure, then to lower it with medication is against His will! If God wants you to have diabetes, then taking insulin is against God's will!

Do you see? Most typically, those who believe their sickness or disease is God's will tend to be the same people who are doing everything they can to escape their sickness or disease. If it's God's will, then enjoy it!

If sickness and disease are NOT God's will, then it makes perfect sense to take medication to alleviate your symptoms while you seek the miraculous healing Jesus purchased.

Paul's advice to Timothy was not an indication of God's will. Rather, it was practical advice given to someone who had not yet been healed.

SPIRITUAL TWEEZERS – Art Thomas

Objection 11
What about Paul Leaving Trophimus Sick in Miletus?

I f God always wants to heal, then why would Paul leave someone in a sick condition?

> **2 Timothy 4:20 –** Erastus stayed in Corinth, and I left Trophimus sick in Miletus. (NIV)

The solution to this objection is very similar to the previous one. The fact that some people remain sick after we pray is not in any way an indication that God intends for them to remain sick forever.

The disciples encountered a young epileptic boy and tried to cast out the demon without results. When the boy was brought to Jesus, however, he was healed. And when the disciples later asked Jesus why they couldn't minister healing to the boy, Jesus told them that it was because of their little faith. (See Matthew 17:14-20.)

When the disciples couldn't bring the freedom God desired, they didn't pat the boy or his father on the back and say, "Well, it may just be God's will for you to have epilepsy. God's ways are mysterious, and we never know what He's saying. In fact, this simply may not be your time, so maybe He's just saying, 'Not yet.'"

No. The disciples didn't say that at all. Rather, stunned that their ministry didn't work, they brought the boy to Jesus, and He accomplished God's will.

Again, based on my experience, it is likely that Paul did try to minister healing to his friend Trophimus and yet didn't see results. Not everyone I minister to receives healing either. But this isn't a revelation of God's will; it's a revelation of the fact that I'm not perfectly like Jesus in His faith.

I'm still growing, and I'm okay with that. Even Paul—who obviously knew Jesus—still expressed a longing to "know Christ and the power of His resurrection." (See Philippians 3:10.)

So this scripture about Paul leaving Trophimus sick in Miletus is not a faith-stopper for me. Rather, it is an encouragement that even Paul had to endure the awkward struggle of people he loved remaining sick despite his belief in God's power to heal.

The fact that not everyone receives salvation does not authorize us to preach that God doesn't always want to save the lost. Our message is that Jesus died for all, and that He therefore deserves all. (See 1 John 2:2.) The same goes for healing. The fact that not everyone is healed does not authorize us to preach that God doesn't always want to heal.

148

On the contrary, our message is that Jesus paid the same price for sickness and disease to be destroyed as He paid for sin to be destroyed. What Jesus did to sin, He did to sickness and disease as well. The same way that His blood purchased salvation for every human being (though not all receive), His blood also purchased healing for every human being (though not all receive).

God's will is to heal. If not, then Jesus would not have paid the price that He paid.

SPIRITUAL TWEEZERS – Art Thomas

Objection 12
What about God's Discipline?

Hebrews teaches us that God "disciplines the one He loves, and He chastens everyone He accepts as His son." (See Hebrews 12:6.) God's discipline is an act of love toward His children that is meant to shape us and produce "a harvest of righteousness." (See Hebrews 12:11.)

Given this, some have used this verse to say that we shouldn't minister healing to someone if their condition is God's discipline. The trouble with this argument is that it isn't consistent with Scripture.

Remember when we talked about Hezekiah. The recently-healed king of Judah felt that his sickness had been the Lord's discipline; but remember that the Lord healed him when he prayed. If Hezekiah's sickness was discipline, God healed him as soon as he cried out for help.

Similarly, remember that when Jesus struck Saul blind on the road to Damascus, the solution was for a Christian to come to him three days later to bring healing. And when Bar-Jesus (Elymas), the sorcerer, was stricken blind, even that was only "for a time."

The implication of Scripture is that if God uses a sickness or disease to discipline someone, then healing is still an expected outcome.

When I discipline my boys, the goal is not the discipline itself. The goal is growth and better actions in the future. If God disciplines someone with a sickness or disease, the goal is not to simply make them sick. The goal is to bring them to a place of wholeness, which includes their physical healing.

But even with those three cases in mind (Hezekiah, Paul, and Elymas), it's also important to know that the word "chasten" in Hebrews 12 means a verbal rebuke or correction. In other words, God's most common way of disciplining and correcting us is just to have a talk with us. Isn't that the example of Scripture? God used prophets to bring verbal correction to His people before He brought down physical consequences.

Furthermore, the trials in this life are not limited to sickness and disease, which means that God has a huge list of other options that He can use to capture our attention and conform us into the image of Christ.

With the exceptions of swift deaths, like Ananias and Sapphira, I cannot find a biblical situation where God's judgment on a person's physical body was not allowed to be healed. Even in the Old Testament, Miriam's leprosy was healed despite it being discipline for challenging God's appointed authority. (See Numbers 12) And while David said, "Because of Your wrath there is no health in my body; there is no soundness in my bones because of my sin," we also see him doing a lot of things throughout his life that prove he was an able-bodied person who wasn't sick forever. (See Psalm 38:3.) Again, Hezekiah's incurable disease was healed when he prayed. And these are only some of the stories.

Have a look at this Old Testament passage:

> **Psalm 107:17-21 –** Some became fools through their rebellious ways and suffered affliction because of their iniquities. They loathed all food and drew near the gates of death. Then they cried to the Lord in their trouble, and He saved them from their distress. He sent out His word and healed them; He rescued them from the grave. Let them give thanks to the Lord for His unfailing love and His wonderful deeds for mankind. (NIV)

In both Old and New Testaments, if God gave sickness as a consequence for sin, healing was always permitted.

This, of course, raises a new question: How do we know when God's discipline is finished and the person is ready to be healed?

Think carefully about this for a moment. If a father spanks his child, the sudden sting and quickly diminishing pain is sufficient to get the point across. He does not need to generate prolonged pain—such an act would be considered abuse. Once the strike of discipline happens, it's over, and God welcomes us back into relationship with Him. If we run from Him and avoid the blessing of His life-giving, healing presence, then that's our own doing. But if we will come to Him humbly, He will restore us. This is seen throughout Scripture.

During the life and ministry of Jesus, we never find Him turning someone away saying that their condition was God's discipline and He wasn't yet through teaching them a lesson. Jesus always healed. Are we to believe that Jesus cut short God's discipline? Or does it make more sense that

Jesus proved that the discipline of the Lord was not a permanent state for His children? Jesus freely forgave and freely healed, and He taught His disciples to do the same. (See Matthew 10:8 and John 20:23.)

This is great news for Christians who want to minister healing. It means that we never have to question whether or not the person in front of us is under God's discipline or whether that might affect the outcome of healing ministry. Throughout the entire ministry of Jesus, we never see God say, "No."

In every situation—even cases of discipline—God's desire is to heal, and He delights in extending the hand of forgiveness even before a person repents. "While we were still sinners, Christ died for us." (See Romans 5:8.)

Objection 13
But Jesus was God!

Perhaps my favorite objection to refute is the assertion that Jesus only healed everyone because He was God, but we shouldn't expect the same results because we're not God.

On a certain level, this is true because we're still growing and being conformed into the likeness of Christ. (See Romans 8:29.) But to suggest that we should never expect to see one-hundred-percent results is frankly unbiblical.

Before we address that issue, I want to point out the illogical nature of this argument. First, the person says it's not always God's will to heal. To this, I respond, "Then why did Jesus heal everyone who came to Him?"

Their answer, of course, is, "Well, Jesus was God! He could do that!"

"So let me get this straight," I answer, "Jesus healed all because He was God, but God doesn't want to heal all?"

Really? Think about that for a second. It doesn't work!

Jesus healed all because the Father wanted to heal all. Jesus didn't go against the will of the Father. Jesus *demonstrated* the will of the Father.

> **John 6:38** – For I have come down from heaven not to do My will but to do the will of Him who sent Me. (NIV)

> **John 8:19b** – ..."If you knew Me, you would know My Father also." (NIV)

> **John 8:28-29** – So Jesus said, "When you have lifted up the Son of Man, then you will know that I am He and that I do nothing on My own but speak just what the Father has taught Me. The One who sent Me is with Me; He has not left Me alone, for I always do what pleases Him."

> **Hebrews 1:3a** – The Son is the radiance of God's glory and the exact representation of his being, sustaining all things by His powerful word.

There is no question about it: Jesus perfectly revealed the Father. So if Jesus healed everyone, it's because He was being consistent with the Father's will.

I want to be clear that I do believe Jesus was and is God in the flesh. The first verse of John's Gospel establishes this. I am convinced that nothing was created apart from Him. (See John 1:3 and Colossians 1:16.) I have no question about the deity of Jesus.

But I also have to recognize that the things Jesus did when He walked this earth, He did not do as God. Rather, He did them as a human being who lived in perfect relationship with the Father. Jesus showed us what it looks like when a human being lives free from sin in right relationship with the Father, and then He paid the full price for us all to be free from sin and in right relationship with the Father. He became like us to make us like Him.

> **Hebrews 2:14-15, 17** – Since the children have flesh and blood, **he too shared in their humanity** so that by his death he might break the power of him who holds the power of death—that is, the devil—and free those who all their lives were held in slavery by their fear of death... **For this reason he had to be made like them, fully human in every way,** in order that he might become a merciful and faithful high priest in service to God, and that he might make atonement for the sins of the people. (NIV)

> **Philippians 2:5-8** – In your relationships with one another, have the same mindset as Christ Jesus: **Who, being in very nature God, did not consider equality with God something to be used to his own advantage;** rather, **he made himself nothing by taking the very nature of a servant**, being made in human likeness. And being found in appearance as a man, he humbled himself by becoming obedient to

death—even death on a cross! (NIV, emphasis
added)

Jesus said that He could do nothing by Himself and
needed to rely on His relationship with the Father. (See John
5:19-21.) He added, "By Myself I can do nothing; I judge
only as I hear, and My judgment is just, for I seek not to
please Myself but Him who sent Me." (See John 5:30.)

Jesus is our perfect example. He showed us what it
looks like when a human being depends on God in perfect
faith. The reason Jesus healed all was not "because He was
God." Even though He *was* God, His consistency in healing
didn't come from His Godhood—it came from His simple
trust in the Father. It came from the fact that the Father had
anointed him with the Holy Spirit and dwelt with Him.

Acts 10:38 – And you know that God anointed
Jesus of Nazareth with the Holy Spirit and with
power. Then Jesus went around doing good and
healing all who were oppressed by the devil, for
God was with him. (NLT)

It doesn't say Jesus healed all because He was God
(even though He was and is). It says Jesus healed all because
God was with Him. And since God is with you too, you
already meet the only qualification! The anointing of the
Holy Spirit that you received from Him abides within you.
(See 1 John 2:27.) That means He never leaves. (See
Matthew 28:20 and Hebrews 13:5.)

Finally, if Jesus healed all because He was God, then
why did the disciples heal all? (See Acts 5:16.) And why did
Paul heal everyone on the island of Malta? (See Acts 28:8-9.)

In the last five years of ministering around the world, I

have—at the time of this writing—been in more than twenty meetings where every single testable condition was healed. Roughly half of those were in America. Others happened in Africa, Europe, and Asia. But in all those cases, I should note, I usually only ministered to one or two people. The results came when all the believers ministered to one another in Jesus' name, and miracles broke out in the room. We are collectively the Body of Christ, and we need to remember that every one of us can do this ministry if we will simply trust Jesus.

Jesus healed everyone because it is the Father's will to heal everyone. And God's will hasn't changed.

John 14:12 – Very truly I tell you, whoever believes in Me will do the works I have been doing, and they will do even greater things than these, because I am going to the Father. (NIV)

1 John 2:6 – Whoever claims to live in him must live as Jesus did. (NIV)

Conclusion to Part Two

In all my experience ministering healing, these are the main biblical objections I hear against God's will to heal all. Any other objections are rare and obscure—and they're all easier to refute than the thirteen I've addressed here.

In other words, you just read reasoned, logical responses to every classic objection against God's will to heal, and none of them had enough weight to truly challenge this standpoint. We didn't even have to abandon the plain reading of the text in order to form these conclusions. If anything, the objections tend to come from assumptions not found in the text itself.

You can have confidence in believing that God's will is always to heal. It's logical, reasoned, and biblically sound.

.

PART

Ten Things Jesus NEVER Said about Healing

SPIRITUAL TWEEZERS – Art Thomas

Introduction to Part Three

You can learn almost as much from the things Jesus never said or did as you can from the things He did say and do—particularly when it comes to healing. Many of the excuses we have formed over time for why some people aren't healed cannot possibly be true because Jesus never used those excuses. Jesus healed every single person who came to Him, called out to Him, or had someone else come to Him on their behalf.

It always worked.

Knowing that it always worked for Jesus is a great challenge to us, especially when we want to dodge personal responsibility for the lack of results. But if healing ministry required the perfect activity on the part of anyone other than Jesus, then He wouldn't have been able to walk in 100% results.

I want to be clear from the beginning of this teaching that while we are supposed to take responsibility for a lack of results (enough to go to Jesus and ask why it didn't work for us when it would have worked for Him, as the disciples did in Matthew 17: 19), we are NOT supposed to carry the burden of a lack of results. It is possible to recognize your own lack of faith and yet not carry the emotional weight of the person's remaining sickness.

If the person is healed, you are to give all the glory to Jesus. And if the person is not healed, you are to give all of the burden to Jesus. All your anxiety and emotional stress needs to be cast onto Jesus because He cares for you. (See 1 Peter 5:7.) To carry that emotional burden around is to be disobedient. Give it up and let the Holy Spirit encourage your heart.

I first preached the content of this section on January 26, 2014 in Jackson, Michigan. As mentioned in this book's Preface, the video of that sermon has now been viewed roughly 15,000 times at the time of this writing. Many have told me how much this information helped them to step into healing ministry with greater confidence.

As I began revising and expanding this book, it occurred to me that this material would be a perfect addition. Naturally, I'm writing this two years after that sermon was first preached, and I've learned a lot more since then. Some of what you read here cannot be found in that message, but it's all based on the original content.

Let's have a look at ten things Jesus never said about healing.

Statement 1

"I'm Sorry, but it's not My Father's will to heal you."

Sometimes, we pray for someone who doesn't show any signs of being healed, and we say well-meaning things like, "You know, God is sovereign, so it's up to Him."

If we believe this way, we will also pray for healing with phrases like, "If it's Your will..." But Jesus never did that. Jesus ministered with confidence about His Father's will.

No one came to Jesus without being healed, and Jesus lived to perfectly reveal the sovereign will of the Father. He never prayed, "If it's Your will..." because He knew the will of the Father.

Yes, God is Sovereign. If He doesn't want to heal someone, then He doesn't have to. Interestingly, He never once exercised that option through the life and ministry of

Jesus. Apparently, our Sovereign God always wants people to be healed. Therefore, if a person remains sick, diseased, or injured after we pray, then something is happening differently than if Jesus were standing there in that moment. Yes, God is sovereign, and our Sovereign God chose to heal all through His Son.

> **Matthew 4:24** – News about him spread all over Syria, and people brought to him all who were ill with various diseases, those suffering severe pain, the demon-possessed, those having seizures, and the paralyzed, and he healed them. (NIV)

> **Matthew 8:16** – When evening came, many who were demon-possessed were brought to him, and he drove out the spirits with a word and healed all the sick. (NIV)

> **Matthew 9:35** – Jesus went through all the towns and villages, teaching in their synagogues, preaching the good news of the kingdom and healing every disease and sickness. (NIV)

> **Matthew 12:15** – Aware of this, Jesus withdrew from that place. Many followed him, and he healed all their sick (NIV)

> **Matthew 14:35-36** – And when the men of that place recognized Jesus, they sent word to all the surrounding country. People brought all their sick to him and begged him to let the sick just touch the edge of his cloak, and all who touched him were healed. (NIV)

Mark 6:56 — And wherever he went — into villages, towns or countryside — they placed the sick in the marketplaces. They begged him to let them touch even the edge of his cloak, and all who touched him were healed. (NIV)

Luke 4:40 — When the sun was setting, the people brought to Jesus all who had various kinds of sickness, and laying his hands on each one, he healed them. (NIV)

Luke 6:18b-19 — ...Those troubled by evil spirits were cured, and the people all tried to touch him, because power was coming from him and healing them all. (NIV)

Acts 10:38 — And you know that God anointed Jesus of Nazareth with the Holy Spirit and with power. Then Jesus went around doing good and healing all who were oppressed by the devil, for God was with him. (NLT)

There is only one case where you could possibly argue that Jesus said it wasn't His Father's will to heal someone.

Matthew 15:22-24 — A Canaanite woman from that vicinity came to him, crying out, "Lord, Son of David, have mercy on me! My daughter is demon-possessed and suffering terribly."

Jesus did not answer a word. So his disciples came to him and urged him, "Send her away, for she keeps crying out after us."

> He answered, "I was sent only to the lost
> sheep of Israel." (NIV)

Jesus essentially said, "My Father sent Me to Israel, not Canaan. It's not My Father's will for me to busy myself with someone who is outside the scope of my mission.

Nevertheless, this woman engaged the Lord in dialogue. And if you know the story, Jesus did heal her daughter. (See Matthew 15:28.) So in the one and only case where you could argue that Jesus sort of said it wasn't His Father's will to heal, Jesus still healed!

As we saw in Part Two, Objection 13, Jesus perfectly revealed the Father's will, and He healed everyone who came to Him. Jesus never questioned God's will about healing. Neither should we.

Statement 2

"I'm Sorry, but My Father is building character in you, so you'll have to remain a leper a while longer."

L et me first clarify that I'm not saying God can't build
your character in the midst of sickness or disease. He
certainly does, since "we know that in all things God works
for the good of those who love him..." (See Romans 8:28.)
He never lets anything go to waste.

But if sickness and disease were God's way of building
character, then why did Jesus go around robbing people of
something that would make them more holy? Why didn't
He go around breaking legs, giving leprosy, and infecting
people with diseases? And remember, Jesus only did what
He saw the Father doing. (See John 5:19.) Apparently the
Father wasn't busy afflicting people with disease either.

The Holy Spirit is fully capable of building our character through His inner work of sanctification—transforming us through the renewal of our minds and conforming us into the likeness of Jesus.

If God needs to use physical means to discipline you and build your character, the New Testament proves that His preferred method is through allowing us to suffer persecution. As proven in Part One, that's the only kind of suffering that Scripture views positively. While God can use a sickness to stop us from doing something terrible (like the sudden blindness of Saul and later Elymas), He doesn't generally use it as a method of character-building. Otherwise, Jesus was working against the Father when He healed all.

Statement 3

"My Father doesn't want to heal you until after you die."

This is an example of a good doctrine that turned into unbiblical advice. When a dear Christian dies while suffering of disease or infirmity, we say that they're now healthy, happy, and dancing in heaven!

Setting aside the debate about when we receive our glorified bodies, let's at least agree with Paul that "to be absent from the body is to be present with the Lord." We do know that in heaven there is no pain, sickness, or disease. If a believer dies of an illness, they're certainly not still sick in heaven with Jesus.

I've heard many people call this "the ultimate healing" because it's more than physical restoration; it's complete newness and perfect health.

I like to say that Jesus believed in "the ultimate healing" too; but thankfully for all the people He ministered to, He never settled for it. When the Bible says on nine occasions that Jesus healed everyone who came to Him, that doesn't mean He killed some of them so that they could be ultimately healed in heaven! (See Matthew 4:24; 8:16; 9:35; 12:15; 14:35-36; Mark 6:56; Luke 4:40; 6:18b-19; and Acts 10:38.)

Statement 4

"I'd like to heal you, but My Father is saying, 'Not yet.' Check with Me again next time I pass through your village."

I've heard people counsel the sick, saying, "Sometimes God's answer to prayer is 'not yet,' so keep trusting and waiting."

That's good advice in most situations. For example, If you're praying for a new job, the Lord might hold off on answering, knowing that the job coming in a few days or weeks will be better than the job you could have right now. But the blood of Jesus didn't pay the price for a new job. And when it comes to those things His blood did pay for, His will is always "yes" and "now."

Have a look at what Isaiah said Jesus purchased:

Isaiah 53:4-5 – Surely He has borne our griefs (sicknesses, weaknesses, and distresses) and carried our sorrows and pains [of punishment], yet we [ignorantly] considered Him stricken, smitten, and afflicted by God [as if with leprosy].

But He was wounded for our transgressions, He was bruised for our guilt and iniquities; the chastisement [needful to obtain] peace and well-being for us was upon Him, and with the stripes [that wounded] Him we are healed and made whole. (AMP)

Jesus' blood paid for both forgiveness and healing. Never would we assume that God's response to a sinner asking for forgiveness is "not yet." On the contrary, we know from Scripture that today is the day of God's favor and salvation. (See 2 Corinthians 6:2.)

The Greek word used in this passage for "salvation" is "*sōtēria.*" It can be translated both as "salvation" and as "health." Similarly, the Greek word used in the New Testament for "save" is "*sōzō,*" which is interchangeably translated into such terms as save, heal, or make whole.

Forgiveness and healing are found coupled together throughout the Bible. For example:

Psalm 103:2-3 – Praise the Lord, my soul, and forget not all his benefits—who forgives all your sins and heals all your diseases. (NIV)

James 5:15 – And the prayer offered in faith will make the sick person well; the Lord will raise them up. If they have sinned, they will be forgiven. (NIV)

And my absolute favorite is found after Jesus forgave the paralyzed man whose friends had lowered him through the roof. The people in the house were baffled that Jesus had just expressed forgiveness to the man.

> **Mark 2:8-12 –** Immediately Jesus knew in his spirit that this was what they were thinking in their hearts, and he said to them, "Why are you thinking these things? Which is easier: to say to this paralyzed man, 'Your sins are forgiven,' or to say, 'Get up, take your mat and walk'? But I want you to know that the Son of Man has authority on earth to forgive sins." So he said to the man, "I tell you, get up, take your mat and go home." He got up, took his mat and walked out in full view of them all. This amazed everyone and they praised God, saying, "We have never seen anything like this!" (NIV)

If forgiveness and healing were not equivalent acts of God based on the same authority and therefore the same principle of Jesus' atonement, then Jesus' act of healing would not have been proof of His authority to forgive. They have to be related in order for this to be proof.

When it comes to the things Jesus purchased with His blood, He always engaged in ministry right away. He freely forgave people. He immediately cast out demons. And He always healed within an hour of ministering to a person, and almost always immediately.

Forgiveness and healing are both important enough to Jesus to pay for them with the same blood. Both are available immediately. "Now is the day of salvation."

SPIRITUAL TWEEZERS – Art Thomas

Statement 5

"Looks like you just don't have enough faith. Bummer."

Jesus raised the dead. Dead people don't have faith. They're dead! In the same way, as long as Jesus had faith, sick people didn't have to. While I know we've already covered this topic at length in Part Two, Objection 7, I want to offer a summary here that will help you directly address this issue.

Whenever we read that Jesus often said, "Your faith has healed you," it's easy to jump to the conclusion that those who aren't healed simply didn't have faith.

There are a few logical inconsistencies here.

First, we never see Jesus say the opposite to someone: "Your lack of faith has drained My power, so you're out of luck." (Again, see the response in Part Two, Objection 7.)

Second, we must remember that it wasn't the person's perfect faith in God that healed them. If that were the case, then they wouldn't have needed to touch Jesus; they would have been already healed by their perfect faith. Instead, they had faith that God would use Jesus to heal them.

Remember, most people didn't realize Jesus was God while He walked among us. Whenever Jesus praised someone for their faith, it was actually their faith in Him to consistently minister healing on behalf of the Father.

I don't know a single sick Christian who doesn't have faith that if they physically touched Jesus, they'd be healed. The problem is that we don't have that faith in each other as the Body of Christ.

The third issue is that Jesus only praised the person's faith about a quarter of the time. The other three quarters of the time, the person's faith wasn't mentioned.

Not all healings happened because of the person's faith in Jesus. The man at the pool of Bethesda didn't even know who Jesus was until He came back and introduced Himself. (See John 5:13-15.) Others were healed because other people had faith on their behalf. (See Matthew 15:28, Mark 2:5-12, and Luke 7:9-10.) And when the epileptic boy wasn't healed, Jesus didn't blame it on the boy's lack of faith or the boy's father's lack of faith; rather, He placed the responsibility squarely on the disciples who were there to represent Him. (See Matthew 17:19-20.)

Faith for healing is not the responsibility of the victim. It is our responsibility as disciples. If someone has faith for their own healing, awesome! That makes my job a lot easier because they'll be healed despite me. But if they don't have faith, this is not an excuse for me to waver in my own faith. My role is to be a part of the Body of Christ, and everyone who touched Jesus' body was healed. (See Matthew 14:36, Mark 6:56, and Luke 6:19.)

As a disciple of Jesus, you have the responsibility to represent Him by having the faith that God will use you (even if no one else thinks He will).

Statement 6

"Too bad your friends and family don't have more faith."

This is similar to the previous point. Especially in cases of terminal illness and extreme suffering, it's terribly difficult for us to watch those we love suffer. And if they died of the disease, it's easy to wonder such things as, "What if I'd had more faith for her to be healed?"

The fact is, God understands the emotional weight carried by the family and doesn't fault us for struggling to speak with faith-filled authority into the situation.

When the disciples couldn't cast the demon out of the epileptic boy, Jesus didn't blame it on the boy's father's lack of faith—even though that same father admitted that he only partially believed. (See Mark 9:24.)

I'm not going to tell you that family members can't minister healing to their loved ones. My wife and I pray for each other and our children all the time and often see immediate results. What I am saying, though, is that God lifts the responsibility from those of us who are emotionally distraught over a loved one's condition, and He instead expects the rest of the Body of Christ to step up and minister the healing He desires. That's one of the reasons we have the Church—to bear one another's weaknesses and stand in faith for those who are weak and struggling. (See Galatians 6:2 and Romans 15:1-3.)

As a matter of fact, when it comes down to the final judgment, Jesus is less concerned with whether or not we ever healed the sick and more concerned with whether or not we cared for them. (See Matthew 7:21-23 and Matthew 25:31-46.) So as long as you're caring for your sick loved one, you're doing the one thing that matters most to the heart of the Lord. Keep seeking healing, but don't allow yourself to feel hopeless or helpless. You're doing everything you're supposed to be doing.

If you have ever prayed for a close family member who died of their condition, I want to release you from any guilt or shame that you've ever felt. The Lord doesn't hold it against you.

Statement 7

"My Father gave you this disease so that I could look more glorious. You need to thank Him for making Me look so good."

I've heard people say that they're grateful to God for their condition because they know it's ultimately for His glory. If there is any Scripture to support this mindset, it is coming from the place where Jesus received word of Lazarus' illness. His reply was, "This sickness will not end in death. No, it is for God's glory so that God's Son may be glorified through it." (See John 11:4.)

The assumption, then, is that some sickness is given by God so that Jesus can be glorified. Yet we often miss two important details: (1) Jesus didn't say God gave the illness;

He said that it would bring glory to God and that He would Himself be glorified; and (2) the way Jesus was glorified was by healing Lazarus when He raised him from the dead!

A similar conclusion is often drawn from the account of Jesus meeting the man who was born blind.

His disciples asked whose sin caused this man to be born blind. But Jesus was clear that the man's blindness wasn't caused by his parents' sin or even by his own. Rather, Jesus clarified, "…this happened so that the works of God might be displayed in him." (See John 9:3.)

A mishandling of this verse over time has produced a theology that assumes God receives glory from our sickness or disease. But that's not what Jesus said. On the contrary, He pointed out that the man's blindness makes an opportunity for God to demonstrate His power. I suppose you could still say that God received glory through the man's blindness, but the way He received glory was by Jesus healing the man!

Can God receive glory while we're still sick and seeking healing? Absolutely. Can He do miraculous things through us even though we're not yet healed? Absolutely. My first two years of practicing healing ministry were done while I was personally suffering with degenerative disc disease. God received glory because I refused to allow my experience to trump my faith in what God wanted. But God received much more glory when He healed me of that disease.

Jesus would rather have what He paid for than have you sick. His blood is not without power, and we should not treat it that way.

Statement 8

"Remember that My kingdom is 'now but not yet,' so not all of you will be healed today."

The idea of God's Kingdom being "now but not yet" is a biblical fact. When people are healed now, they still eventually die, awaiting the future resurrection when the dead in Christ will rise first and then those who are living will be caught up with them. (See 1 Thessalonians 4:16-17.) Only at that time will we have our eternal, glorified bodies like Jesus now has. (See 1 Corinthians 15.) The fullness of God's Kingdom has not yet been established, but it is nevertheless accessible now in various forms.

The important thing to realize is that Jesus healed people according to the "now" of the Kingdom—not the "not yet." Jesus healed all, and yet His Kingdom had not yet fully come.

While there are some things we don't enjoy now (like eternal, glorified bodies), physical healing is a blessing that can *only* be experienced now. After all, what good is physical healing to an eternal, glorified body? We have no use for physical healing in the future Kingdom. It's a tool that's available today and is in the hands of every citizen of Jesus' Kingdom.

When people say that "the Kingdom is now but not yet," they're right. But when they use it as an excuse for why some people aren't healed, they ignore that Jesus was healing everyone two thousand years ago! Physical healing for all is part of the "now" Kingdom, and it should be seen as such.

Statement 9

"We need to figure out the spiritual roots of this sickness or this just isn't going to work."

Sometimes people receive healing as they repent of sin. I know a woman who was healed of cancer after forgiving her mother and sister and repenting of her bitterness. This doesn't mean that all sickness is caused by sin, but some certainly is.

The question, though, is whether or not we need to identify the underlying sin issue in order for the person to be healed. The answer, biblically, is "no."

When James wrote about healing, he said, "...the prayer offered in faith will make the sick person well; the Lord will raise them up. If they have sinned, they will be forgiven." (See James 5:15.) I like to say that the blood of

Jesus is messy—get a little on you for healing, and it will minister forgiveness too. The same goes the other way as well: Apply the blood for forgiveness, and healing is also likely. (I should note here, however, that a lack of physical healing is not proof of a lack of forgiveness). Notice the next verse James writes. This time, confession of sin comes first and healing is second. (See James 5:16.) There's no formula; just Jesus.

While Jesus did—at least on one occasion—minister forgiveness before ministering healing, He didn't specifically identify the man's sins. (See Mark 2:5-12.) In fact, this passage seems to imply that the healing was proof of His authority, not a result of the man's forgiveness.

Jesus regularly ministered healing without stipulations. He never required repentance first. After Jesus healed the invalid at the pool of Bethesda, He said to the man, "See, you are well again. Stop sinning or something worse may happen to you." (See John 5:14.) Healing came first, and repentance wasn't even necessarily guaranteed.

So while it is true that some are healed after confessing and repenting of sin, it is also true that those who are healed are simultaneously forgiven (leaving the person free to choose repentance). There is no requirement for which must come first.

When we stand ministering healing, it is important that we be free from doubt. If we think that the person might have a hidden sin that is hindering their healing, then we won't pray with faith. Jesus never concerned Himself with such things. He simply ministered healing.

Statement 10

"Unfortunately, this sickness is a punishment for your sin, and you have to reap what you've sown."

This statement is similar to Part Two, Objection 12. As I already outlined there, if God used a sickness or disease as discipline (as He did for Paul and for Elymas), His will is still healing. There's no such thing in the New Testament as an ongoing, chronic, punishment from God.

Let's take one more look at the prophet Isaiah's words:

> **Isaiah 53:4a** – Surely He has borne our griefs (sicknesses, weaknesses, and distresses) and carried our sorrows and pains [of punishment]...

Even if your pain is punishment from the Lord, He wants you to be healed.

As we've noted several times, the only person in the New Testament who we can clearly say that Jesus personally made sick was Saul on the road to Damascus. Jesus struck him blind. But what happened 3 days later? A Christian ministered healing. This Christian didn't have the power or authority to trump the will of God. Rather, he illustrated it. Besides that, Saul was an enemy of the Gospel, murdering Christians. Unless you're murdering Christians, you probably didn't receive your sickness or disease from God.

> **Isaiah 53:5a** – But He was wounded for our transgressions... (AMP)

Any wounding you deserve for your transgressions, Jesus took.

> **Isaiah 53:5b** – ...He was bruised for our guilt and iniquities... (AMP)

Any bruising you deserve for your guilt and iniquities, Jesus took.

> **Isaiah 53:5c** – ...the chastisement [needful to obtain] peace and well-being for us was upon Him... (AMP)

If you think you need to be physically punished for the sake of your peace and well-being, I have good news for you: Jesus took that too.

> **Isaiah 53:5d** – ...and with the stripes [that wounded] Him we are healed and made whole. (AMP)

The beauty of the cross is that a divine exchange occurred. Jesus reaped what we have sown, and we reap what He has sown.

- ❖ We sowed sin, and He reaped death.
- ❖ He sowed perfection and innocence, and we reap eternal life.
- ❖ We sowed evil, and He reaped evil.
- ❖ He sowed love, mercy, and grace; and we reap sonship.
- ❖ We murdered the Son of God, and he received the torture.
- ❖ He poured out His perfect, innocent blood, and we received vindication.

The things we receive in Christianity are the things Jesus deserves. And the things Jesus received at the cross are the things we deserve. The purpose of Jesus' death was to reconcile man to God. It was to restore the beautiful relationship which was lost when sin entered the world.

If you've managed to read this far into this book and only now realize that you've never given your life to Jesus, now is a good time. Thank Him for His sacrifice, receive His forgiveness, believe that His is alive today, and surrender to His Lordship over all. Talk to Him like you would talk to anyone, and ask Him to give you His Holy Spirit to live inside of you right now. You will experience the transformational, saving power of the Lord.

SPIRITUAL TWEEZERS – Art Thomas

Conclusion to Part Three

Whenever you hear someone avoid personal responsibility and make an excuse for why God didn't heal someone, ask whether or not that's something Jesus ever said. Most of the time, it's easy to refute any excuse this way.

I can think of plenty of other things Jesus never said about healing. Here are ten more for example:

- ❖ "Wow...That's a tough disease. Hang tight while I go pray and fast for three days."
- ❖ "Unfortunately, healing is for Christians, so you need to be saved first."

- ❖ "Pray for Me, guys. I laid hands on that guy too hastily, and now I'm being attacked."
- ❖ "Now, everyone form a nice, tidy line because the Holy Spirit won't move if there's disorder."
- ❖ "Turns out you were serving demons by going to so many doctors. You can't be healed."
- ❖ "Oh, God, I beg You to have pity on this poor soul."
- ❖ "Please give Judas your money first, and then we'll talk about your healing."
- ❖ "I can't do this one without some olive oil… Get the scented stuff, Peter."
- ❖ "I know you're still having symptoms, but you just need to believe you're healed."
- ❖ "Ooh…yeah… Amputated body parts are impossible to heal. Sorry."

So what DID Jesus say? Obviously, I'm not going to list every little thing Jesus said in the Gospels. You can read the Bible yourself for that! However, I do want you to see one particular statement as it pertains to healing:

> **Matthew 10:1,7-8** – Jesus called his twelve disciples to him and gave them authority to drive out impure spirits and to heal every disease and sickness… "As you go, proclaim this message: 'The kingdom of heaven has come near.' Heal the sick, raise the dead, cleanse those who have leprosy, drive out demons. Freely you have received; freely give." (NIV)

Admittedly, this command was given to the Twelve— not to every single follower of Jesus. However, when Jesus commissioned these same Twelve in Matthew 28:18-20, He added that when they make disciples, they are to teach the new converts "to obey everything I have commanded you." Thus everything Jesus commanded the Twelve has also been commanded of us. Therefore, He has also given you and me the "authority to drive out impure spirits and to heal every disease and sickness."

Jesus told us to go heal the sick—not some of the sick, but *the* sick. Period. If a person is sick (meaning weak, diseased, or infirmed in any way), then you are fully authorized as a disciple of Jesus to minister healing. Healing ministry is not a matter of figuring out God's will for each person. Rather, healing ministry is a matter of obedience to the command of Jesus Christ, who proved the Father's will through His example and sacrifice.

Never allow the things Jesus never said to hinder what God wants to do through you. You are a disciple of Jesus. Now, go heal the sick in His name!

As you go about ministering healing to the people in your life, you're sure to meet some who will want to debate your convictions. These are generally well-meaning people who want to spare people from false-hopes and don't want to diminish God's glory (as if we really could). Don't be afraid to engage the debate, but do it all in humility. This book has prepared you for the task.

1 Peter 3:15b – ...Always be prepared to give an answer to everyone who asks you to give the reason for the hope that you have. But do this with gentleness and respect. (NIV)

Don't let doubt creep in. Whenever you have doubts, read this book again. As time goes on, your mind will be renewed, and you'll remain convinced of God's will to heal.

SPIRITUAL TWEEZERS – Art Thomas

APPENDIX:

Core Practices for Ministering Healing

by Art Thomas

Originally Published in the
PAID IN FULL 40-Day Healing Ministry Activation Manual,
Supernatural Truth Productions, LLC

There is no set method for conducting healing ministry, but there are some general principles that are helpful tools when you're unsure what to do next.

Wherever the word "minister" is used in this section, it refers to laying hands on the person and/or speaking a word of authority. These principles are a "default" of sorts, based on the example of Jesus and His disciples in the Bible. If the Holy Spirit instructs you to do something else, then obedience to His voice becomes the form of ministry.

The following list of "core practices" are titled as such because they are the foundation on which successful healing ministry can function. None of these principles is a requirement for seeing healing, but we have found them to be helpful in the actual practice of healing ministry. Our hope in presenting them here is to offer very practical advice that will help you experience success in healing ministry and avoid some of the problems from which we have learned.

Relational Approach

Keep things friendly, non-threatening, and upbeat. Smile. Look the person in the eye. Ask permission to lay hands on the person. Feel free to explain what you're doing or chat with the person while you lay hands on them. All of the cultural things we often like to do as Pentecostals or Charismatics during healing ministry (like shouting, jumping, speaking in tongues, shaking, pushing, etc.) are completely unnecessary when it comes to what brings results. You can be very quiet, happy, and "ordinary" and still see God do the miraculous through you.

Test the Condition

Before you begin, ask if there are any symptoms that, if they went away, the person would know they're healed.

In many cases, there is an immediate symptom that can be tested: pain, blindness, deafness, immobility, etc. In these instances, begin with a baseline assessment. If it's pain, for instance, ask them to rate the pain on a scale of one to ten (something many people are used to doing for doctors). If it's blurry eyesight, ask them to look around for something they can test their vision on. How far can they see now? Establish what the person cannot currently do, and then begin ministry.

After ministering to the person, ask them to test their condition. How does it compare? Has there been any change?

One of my favorite questions is, "Is it 100% complete?" Many people will be so happy to have relief that they are satisfied with a partial healing. I tell people that Jesus paid for 100%, and He deserves 100%; then I continue to minister and test things again until the person says their symptoms are completely gone.

In some cases, a condition cannot be tested immediately (like digestive tract issues, allergies, asthma, internal cancer, or diabetes). In these instances, simply minister once, and then ask the person how they feel. Ask them to check their condition later (seeing a doctor if appropriate) and to let you know what happens.

Keep Things Short

Long prayers are almost always unnecessary. In fact, I've learned that in most cases, the faster I minister, the better. Jesus warned us not to pray like the pagans who think they'll be heard because of their many words (Matthew 6:7-8).

In fact, be open to the possibility of God healing a person before you even have the opportunity to minister to them. Listen for the Holy Spirit to prompt you about these scenarios and learn to call them out by asking the person if they're already healed.

Simply place a hand on the person, command the

healing briefly, and have the person test it out right away. You'll be amazed how many healings happen that quickly. This also helps keep ministry from taking forever if we find that we need to minister more than once to the person.

Recognizing What God is Doing

Occasionally when I'm ministering healing to someone and I ask them what's happening, they will tell me that they feel heat or electricity around their affected body part (or sometimes throughout their entire body). When this happens, I tell them, "Good. It sounds like God is doing something. So we're just going to let Him do what He's doing, and you can let me know when the sensation stops.

If I'm ministering in a meeting where multiple people are waiting for prayer, I'll use this as an opportunity to pray for someone else. I'll instruct the person to wait there and let God keep working while I pray for someone else, and I assure them that I'll check back in a moment. Every so often, while ministering to the second person, I'll ask the first, "What's happening?" to keep a running assessment of their condition.

When I'm not in a meeting and am alone with the person or on the streets somewhere, I'll usually keep my hand on the area being affected and use the time to chat with the person, explain what's happening, or share the Gospel.

Typically, once God takes over in this way, there's nothing left for me to do. He'll complete the healing without my help. But such experiences with the fiery or electric power of God can sometimes be scary for the person, so my presence becomes a reassuring reminder that things are still under control and everything is okay.

Model Gratitude

Every time you see the least bit of change, verbally thank the Lord for what He's doing. This will teach the person to express their own gratitude to God whenever they experience the slightest improvement. I have seen many times when a healing was completed while we were still thanking Him. In fact, I know many people who use gratitude as their preferred method of ministering healing (you may remember Josh MacDonald in our movie grabbing a man's ankle and saying, "Thank You, Father, for a brand new ankle in Jesus' name").

What to do When Pain Moves or Intensifies

Of the thousands of healings I've witnessed, I've seen more than a hundred situations where the pain in the person's body moved from one place to another. Whenever this happens, we know that it's not a normal medical condition. Rather, a demon is behind it, and it just tried to escape what God was doing in one area by scurrying to another.

On a few occasions, I've seen the pain intensify. One woman came to me with fibromyalgia, and when I started to minister to her, the pain became so unbearable that she couldn't stand. I grabbed a chair for her and continued to minister. She cried, "It's too much! I want to stop!" I replied, "I can leave you in this condition if that's what you want, but wouldn't you rather be free?" After about four or five minutes telling the spirit to leave, it came out, and the woman was completely relieved.

Any time the pain moves or intensifies in response to healing ministry, it's a dead giveaway that a demon is at work. When that happens, immediately command the spirit to leave, and ask the person what's happening.

If it moves again or intensifies again, then command it to leave again. Repeat this until it's complete (see Appendix F for more information).

If the symptoms stop, alleviate, or remain the same, I assume that the demon is gone and return to ministering healing. Many times after telling a demon to leave, the person's pain remained the same, but I was then able to tell the affected part to be healed and see results.

Using Words of Knowledge

There are many expressions and uses of the spiritual gift known as a "Word of Knowledge." If you're particularly interested in studying this topic, please refer to the book I wrote titled *The Word of Knowledge in Action: A Practical Guide for the Supernatural Church*, published by Destiny Image Publishers, 2011.

For the purposes of this study on healing ministry, this brief crash course will be sufficient.

A Word of Knowledge happens when the Holy Spirit takes something Jesus knows and makes it known to you. One of the ways He does this in healing ministry is to cause you to become aware of a particular body part by causing you to feel warmth, tingling, or occasionally even pain in the same area where the person is affected. Another way is simply through information dropped in your mind that you somehow know without any earthly explanation as to why you know it.

Words of Knowledge are extremely useful in healing

ministry. One of their greatest values is that they build faith in both the person receiving ministry and in you as the minister. Furthermore, acting on a Word of Knowledge is an expression of obedience, which positions you in submission to God, allowing His authority to flow freely through you.

Obedience producing authority is the whole point. We know that God wants to heal every person in the room, but He sometimes gives a Word of Knowledge so that we have a practical opportunity to submit ourselves to Him in obedience. Whenever I call out a condition through a Word of Knowledge, I know that healing will happen—not because God just told me the only condition He wants to heal but because I know I'm honoring the flow of authority by yielding in obedience to Him. This positions me to speak with His authority and see the healing take place.

Knowing When and How to Back Off

There are seven basic reasons to stop a healing ministry session:

1) The person is healed.
2) The person asks you to stop.
3) You can tell that the person is wanting to stop but is perhaps trying to be polite, so you offer them a way out and they take it.
4) The schedule or venue requires for you to stop or move on.
5) The Holy Spirit is specifically telling you to do something else.
6) You're exhausted physically and emotionally and recognize your own need to rest.

7) You notice that you've stepped outside of faith and started striving in your own effort or pride (trying to achieve results for the sake of looking good, feeling good, or some other selfish reason), and you recognize that you're unable to snap out of it.

The first five scenarios are fairly straightforward to navigate. The last two leave you with some options.

My first act is usually to bring in reinforcements. I'll either ask the Holy Spirit to bring someone to my attention, or I'll simply ask the first person I see if they want to try. Often times, I'll see if there's a little child standing by, and I'll ask if they would like to try. Kids usually jump at the opportunity even when they've been watching things not work for you.

Whoever you have take over for you, coach them through the process and show them what to do. In most cases, I've seen healing work after this.

As a final resort, I'll look the person in the eye and say, "Alright. I'm recognizing that I'm not ministering in faith right now for some reason. If Jesus had touched you, you'd be healed by now; instead, I touched you. But I am absolutely convinced that God wants you to be healed. So I want to encourage you to have Christians continue to minister to you until you're 100% free. You can even speak to the condition yourself. If you want me to keep trying, I'd be happy to, but I need to be honest when I'm recognizing my own moments of weakness."

Ministering to Children

Imagine being a helpless child who's not feeling well physically. Mom or dad scoops you up, and—usually with concern on their face—carries you to a total stranger who lays hands on you and starts shouting in a language you don't know. That's a terrifying experience!

As the minister, there are several things you can do to eliminate the intimidation factor and put the child at ease.

First, smile. Greet the child with an excited expression and say, "Hi there!"

If the child is walking when they're brought to you, immediately stoop down to a kneeling position so that they can meet you on their level.

If the child is vocal enough, try to engage in a little small talk. Tell them your name and ask for theirs. Notice any toys they might be carrying or perhaps a character on their clothing. Then ask with a smile, "What can I pray for you about?"

Many times, the parents will explain the situation. If you're on the ground with the child, stay there and look up at the parents. Whether the parents or the child explain the condition, look back to the child and ask them, "How do you feel right now?" This will help you establish your baseline for testing later. If it's not a testable condition, it will at least express that you care for the child.

Ask the child if it's okay for you to put your hand on them. Be specific about where you intend to place your hand. Then ask the parents, "Is that alright?"

If it's not okay with either the child or the parents, don't worry about it, and move on.

Still smiling, happy, and looking the child in the eye, speak words of authority to the condition in soft, gentle tones. Sicknesses and demons are not intimidated by the volume or intensity of your voice; they're intimidated by the fact that you sit on the throne with Jesus (Ephesians

2:6). There is no need to minister fear to a child while you're trying to minister healing!

If the condition can be tested, ask the child if they want to test it out. Some are very shy and want to stay clinging to mom or dad, and that's okay. In these cases, I tell the parents, "That's fine. Have her check it out later, and if the problem is still there, do the same thing I just did and check it out again."

When finished, thank the child for letting you pray for him or her. Tell them that they did a great job. And whenever the child will go for it, try to end with a high-five, fist-bump, or hand shake.

About the Author

Art Thomas is a missionary-evangelist who has preached the Gospel in diverse settings spanning from the inner city of Brooklyn, New York, to the bush of Africa. Now serving as the president and CEO of Wildfire Ministries International, Art has seen hundreds of people come to salvation and thousands physically healed. He is the director and producer of the movies *Paid in Full* and *Voice of God* and has been actively involved in training tens of thousands of believers to minister in the power of the Holy Spirit since 2009. He lives with his wife, Robin, and their two boys, Josiah and Jeremiah, in Plymouth, Michigan.

SPIRITUAL TWEEZERS – Art Thomas

Art's First Book

The Word of Knowledge in Action is a book that removes the traditional confusion surrounding the spiritual gift known as a word of knowledge. In this text, Art shares testimonies, biblical insights, and practical advice that will train and equip you for active supernatural ministry.

Pastor Bill Johnson, author of *When Heaven Invades Earth*, and lead pastor at Bethel Church in Redding, California, writes:

> Art Thomas' book, *The Word of Knowledge in Action*, speaks of a lifestyle that is both practical and powerful—and ultimately available to every believer. He shares wonderful personal stories and insights that help to create great hunger in readers. These stories connect readers with their own ability to hear and activate them to walk in this gift in everyday experiences. *The Word of Knowledge in Action* is a timely book, as God is releasing His Church in a fresh and powerful way of bringing people into an experience with God.

Your copy of *The Word of Knowledge in Action* can be purchased through bookstores everywhere or at www.SupernaturalTruth.com.

The Word of Knowledge in Action, by Art Thomas, is published by Destiny Image Publishers.

SPIRITUAL TWEEZERS – Art Thomas

Invite Art Thomas
to Speak at
Your Church or Event

Art Thomas is available for speaking engagements at churches, conferences, seminars, and other events. He preaches and teaches about healing ministry, identity in Christ, supernatural evangelism, and more. His heart is to train and equip Christians everywhere to live like Jesus in attitude, action, and power.

You can view Art's itinerary and find out more info at www.ArtThomas.org.

SPIRITUAL TWEEZERS – Art Thomas

About the Movie:
PAID IN FULL

Imagine what would happen if every Christian was equipped to minister physical healing the way Jesus did. That's God's plan for the Church!

In Acts 5:12 and 16, we learn that the believers all met together in a part of the Temple called Solomon's Colonnade, and every sick and tormented person who came to them was healed. In the ministry of Jesus, everyone who touched His body was healed. (See Matthew 14:35-36; Mark 6:56; Luke 4:40; and Luke 6:18-19.) Now, WE are His Body! (See 1 Corinthians 12:27.)

PAID IN FULL is a film about God's continued desire to heal the sick, the diseased, the infirmed, the disabled, and the injured through ordinary people just like you. Meet more than 30 people who practice Christian healing ministry, and:

- o Witness instant miracles happening in public,
- o Hear testimonies of medically-documented healings, and
- o Learn how you too can minister healing in Jesus' name!

Experience a movie like none other. Discover more than what is happening throughout the world; JOIN IN!

Order your copy today at:
www.SupernaturalTruth.com

Please consider sharing this book with a friend and writing a
review on Amazon.com. Each Amazon review (positive or
negative) increases the likelihood of people finding this book
online. Thank you!

Additional copies available at
www.SupernaturalTruth.com